Leaving the stream, we now struggled
up the bank through dense jungle
and in a few minutes reached the
bottom of a very precipitous slope.
For an hour and twenty minutes
we had a hard climb....

*The Urubamba River
near Machu Picchu.*

Richarte and Alvarez sent a small boy with me as a "guide." He urged us to climb up a steep hill over what seemed to be a flight of stone steps. We came to a narrow stairway made of large granite blocks. Only a very small man could have passed along it in the time of the Incas!

We set up our camp just above this house.

Early afternoon.

Our young guide.

Our guide led us along one of the widest terraces, and we made our way into an untouched forest beyond. Suddenly I found myself confronted with the walls of ruined houses built of the finest quality Inca stone work. It was hard to see them, for they were partly covered with trees and moss, the growth of centuries. But in the dense shadow, hiding in bamboo thickets and tangled vines, appeared here and there walls of white granite ashlars carefully cut and exquisitely fitted together. What a marvel!

September 1911. Start of the excavation.

The clearance work has begun at Machu Picchu. Here, in the great temple, Lieutenant Sotomayor (on the right) directs the group of native workers.

This must be more or less how the huge Inca jars were carried.

Inca designs found on potsherds.

We found this magnificent bronze knife ornamented with a figure of a fisherman (opposite).

Cave no. 9 is one of the largest funerary caves. On its floor we found numerous skeletons…and fragments

of marvelous pots that must have been placed there with the dead.

In cave no. 11, Dr. Eaton, a specialist in osteology, is uncovering a human skeleton. On the right is a soldier generously "lent" by the Peruvian government to guarantee the security of the workers.

These rectangular houses are built of ashlars wedged with small irregular stones called "pachillas."

This roofing technique is still used by present-day Quechuas.

Here is one of the communal houses that made up the former city. There were several clans or families which each possessed from six to sixteen houses. Each cluster of dwellings is markedly different from the others. This one, for example, displays a very particular type of stone masonry.

This was the closing mechanism for doors, as far as we can gather from the surviving bolting system.

The houses probably had no furniture! In some, however, we found big flat stones that may have served as beds. And in a few corners there were stone seats, like this one.

May 1912.

In one house we found a mortar, doubtless used for grinding maize or dried potatoes. Next to it was a big stone used as a pestle. Our guide placed pestle on mortar exactly as though he were going to prepare a meal of maize for today.

Here is a group of sacred rocks surrounded by terraces. On the upper level, the stones reach extraordinary dimensions. Some are as tall as a man. One wonders how the Incas could move them without wheels or draft animals.… It would have required a healthy dose of naïveté —and a small army of workers—to move these enormous rocks.

Machu Picchu in the process of being excavated. It is hard to imagine the final result.

One of the 1912 expedition's first topographical surveys.

The excavation has wrought wonders.
The hill of the *intihuatana* and the
terraces to the west of the sacred
plaza have at last emerged
from the forest.

*On the left,
vertiginous precipices, and down
below, the Urubamba River foams
and rumbles.*

The sacred city was well and
truly impregnable!

CONTENTS

I IN SEARCH OF EL DORADO
13

II THE PASSION OF ATAHUALPA
31

III EVERYDAY LIFE AND WORK
55

IV THE ERADICATION OF IDOLATRY
73

V THE INCA'S RETURN
93

VI THE HERITAGE OF THE INCAS
113

DOCUMENTS
129

Map
184

Further Reading
185

List of Illustrations
185

Index
189

THE INCAS
PEOPLE OF THE SUN

Carmen Bernand

DISCOVERIES®

ABRAMS, NEW YORK

In 1511 a rumor began to circulate among the Spanish settlers in Panama that several days' journey to the south of the isthmus there stretched a vast kingdom, a fabulous country of untold riches. When this news reached the ears of Spanish explorer Vasco Núñez de Balboa (1475–1519), discoverer of the Pacific Ocean, it sounded like a challenge.

CHAPTER I

IN SEARCH OF EL DORADO

By the 19th century, the Incas had become a Romantic legend. Left: Wallpaper manufactured in 1826 showing the Incas worshiping the setting sun. Right: A 16th-century ship, comparable to those in which Pizarro and his companions sailed to Peru.

Exasperated by the greed of the foreigners who had settled in Panama under Balboa's leadership, a native chief exhorted the intruders to go farther south in search of the gold after which they lusted so much. He claimed that a mysterious southern kingdom had so much of the precious metal that the people there used it to make even the most ordinary objects (hence the Spanish name for the mythical land, El Dorado, "the gilded"). Balboa made several attempts to reach the fabled land; it was on one such attempt, in 1513, that he sighted the Pacific Ocean. But the explorer was the victim of a plot contrived by a rival Spanish conquistador, Pedrarias Dávila, and was condemned to death and executed without fulfilling the dream that these tales had aroused in him.

A few years later, in 1522, Spanish adventurer Pascual de Andagoya (c. 1495–1548) undertook a more fruitful expedition to the south. The voyage was quite brief, but during the trip Andagoya heard from native merchants a great deal of very detailed testimony about an immensely rich empire that lay hundreds of miles to the south.

The accounts of the conquistadors often failed to convey a very accurate image to European readers. This illustration by an artist of the Netherlands depicts the inhabitants of Peru as half-naked savages. The French map opposite shows several fantastic creatures.

Intrigued by Andagoya's Reports, Two Conquistadors Began to Dream of Finding El Dorado

Conquistadors Francisco Pizarro (c. 1476–1541), who had accompanied Balboa on his 1513 expedition, and Diego de Almagro (c. 1475–1538) lacked the means to undertake privately such an expedition, with its steep costs and uncertain outcome. So they joined forces with a Roman Catholic priest from Panama, Hernando de Luque, who agreed to give them financial support for the conquest (against the advice of Dávila, who had been made governor of Panama after Balboa's death). Two vessels were chartered, and, in 1524, a first expedition set sail—but with no success. The two boats sailed along the rainy coast of South

America, which was covered with mangroves (tropical evergreen trees) and infested with mosquitoes. This land bore no resemblance to the El Dorado eulogized by Andagoya, although from time to time the Spaniards met a few natives who wore golden jewelry and told of a powerful kingdom to the south. But partway down the coast of what is today the country of Colombia, the Spaniards discovered a tribe of cannibals. Horrified, they gave up and returned to Panama.

Pizarro and his comrades are shown on board their ship (left), in a drawing made in the late 16th century by Felipe Guamán Poma de Ayala—a man of both Spanish and Inca descent who left an unusual illustrated record of Inca life. The natives themselves traveled in large seagoing rafts, such as the one shown below.

The First Meeting Between the Spaniards and the Inhabitants of the Andean Cordillera

A second expedition, in 1526–7, was more promising. While Pizarro stayed on land at the mouth of the river now known as the San Juan, his navigator, Bartolomé Ruiz, sailed on southward. Ruiz had almost reached the border of present-day Ecuador when he saw a sailing vessel like a raft coming toward him. This was the first boat the Spaniards had encountered in these waters. On board this raft were men and women, all dressed in superb, richly embroidered woolen fabrics that inspired the Europeans' admiration. Using the interpreters he had brought with him, Ruiz learned that the vessel came from a port called Tumbes, located at the modern border of Peru and Ecuador.

After explaining to the Spaniards that the fine wool of their clothes came from llamas, camel-like animals of which there were numerous herds in their country, the natives confirmed that gold abounded there, too. They also mentioned the name of Huayna Capac, the "Great

Inca" (also referred to simply as "the Inca"), whom they identified as sovereign of the entire region. Ruiz took a few of the natives on board with him, and then he rejoined Pizarro.

Too few in number to attempt any use of force in the mountainous lands they would have to traverse, the conquistadors sent some of their group back to seek reinforcements in Panama. Pizarro and his men awaited them on the Isla del Gallo. But when the ship finally came back, the men who had remained with Pizarro—exhausted by the long and difficult wait—expressed their desire to return to Panama without even attempting to explore the regions to the south. Only Pizarro remained fiercely determined. Facing his dispirited companions, he drew a line on the

The manufacture of textiles, a key component of all Andean civilizations, had begun in Paracas, in ancient Peru, more than ten centuries before the establishment of the Inca empire. Above: A textile of the Paracas culture.

ground and declared, "Comrades and friends, on this side lie poverty, hunger, effort, torrential rains, and privation. On that side lies pleasure. On this side, we return to Panama and poverty. On that side, we become rich." Twelve of his companions were persuaded. History has immortalized these explorers by the name the "Thirteen of the Isla del Gallo."

A portrait of Pizarro by Vasquez Diaz Trujillo.

It was in fighting the Moors, nomadic peoples of northern Africa who settled in the Spanish region of Granada, that the Spanish learned how to counter what is today known as guerrilla warfare. This experience, together with the superiority of their weaponry (above left, a Spanish sword and scabbard), was to prove advantageous in Peru.

The Spaniards were equipped with lances and arquebuses (left). (The arquebus is a pre-decessor of the musket.)

At first the Spaniards did not succeed in penetrating the vast territory of the Andes and had to content themselves with looking at what they believed to be El Dorado from the sea. Sailing along the coast, they could just make out the imposing outline of Chimborazo. This 20,561-foot-high volcano in central Ecuador is visible from the sea in fine weather, despite the distance. As they progressed southward, the snowcapped mountains of the Andes became clearer, forming a seemingly impassable barrier between the foreigners and the Great Inca's country.

When they reached Tumbes, a port with heavy seagoing traffic, the adventurers were greeted by the locals with kindness. Charmed by the beauty of the native women, one of the Spaniards, Alonzo de Molina, decided to remain on land. The description that he later gave his comrades of the riches he had seen was extraordinary.

The Inca's army may have numbered more than 200,000 men, armed with bows, arrows, clubs, spears, and slings (below, a colored engraving of 1572). The soldiers wore padded jerkins that were more effective against arrows than against arquebus shots.

Laughter and Exchanges of Gifts: The Conquest Proceeded Almost Like a Good-natured Festival

Out of the smiling throng suddenly stepped a person of distinction, whose serious air contrasted with the generally relaxed attitude. This was one of the Great Inca's *orejónes* ("big ears"), so named by the Spaniards because the earlobes of all the Inca's ambassadors were disfigured by heavy ornaments. This dignitary inquired about the Spaniards' intentions. What had they come to seek in these countries so far from their own? When Pizarro spoke to him of the great Charles V of Spain, the "most powerful emperor in the world," the dignitary said nothing. He accepted the gift of an ax of iron, a metal as yet unknown to the people of the Andes (or indeed to anyone in the Americas), and then he discreetly dispatched a messenger to Quito (an important Inca capital), where Huayna Capac was visiting, to inform the Inca of the arrival of these disturbing men.

Delighted by their welcome, the Spaniards sailed on as

"On this side poverty, on that side riches" —Pizarro's famous moment of choice as seen by a 19th-century artist (below). Those who followed Pizarro were men of humble origin, whose later pretensions to nobility were founded purely on bloodshed.

far as Chincha, on the southern coast of present-day Peru. There they came upon desert shores that had been used as immense cemeteries. After a brief exploration of this area they headed northward once more. Passing Tumbes again, they took three young boys along with them, with the aim of teaching them Spanish. One of these was a certain Felipillo, who was to play a decisive role in the history of the conquest.

Sailing from port to port, the Spaniards learned that in fact the Great Inca reigned over a mosaic of peoples who only recently had been subjugated. Indeed, when the conquistadors arrived, the Inca empire was little more than a century old. Its territory extended northward to the province of Pasto (south of modern Colombia) and southward to the Maule River, in central Chile. Within this immense expanse lived a great variety of peoples who had been integrated in varying ways into the whole.

At puberty, Inca boys of royal lineage underwent a rite of passage called *huarachico*, during which their earlobes were perforated. This ritual entitled them to become warriors and to learn of the exploits of past dynasties. The period of initiation lasted from October to December and included mortifications of the flesh and seclusion on the sacred mountain of Huanacauri. This tradition of the *orejónes* still exists today in a modified form (above).

How the Incas Built up Such a Vast Empire So Quickly Remains an Enigma

The enigma is made all the more insoluble by the fact that the history of the successive dynasties and their victories often is little more than legend. Although it has become apparent that the powerful families from which the Incas descended were originally established around Cuzco (which became the capital of the Inca empire), in the heart of the Andean Cordillera, it is difficult to retrace precisely the chronological and political stages that led from the Cuzco confederation to the Inca empire. According to the accounts gathered by Europeans from actual members of the family of the Inca Huascar (Huayna Capac's successor), it was the Inca emperor Pachacuti who, in the 15th century, had built the formidable empire that dazzled the Spaniards.

The people of Cuzco referred to their empire as Tahuantinsuyu, the "Land of the Four Quarters," a name that was both symbolic and administrative: The empire was arranged around Cuzco, the "navel," in

The Incas built citadels, *pucara*, throughout the empire. The most majestic fortress, that of Sacsahuaman, still overlooks the town of Cuzco. It is surrounded by a wall of stones that are so well fitted that a knife blade cannot be inserted between them. In Inca times the fortress was defended by three towers that were connected to the Inca's palace by underground passages.

four sectors oriented to each of the cardinal points. To the north lay Chinchaysuyu, which encompassed all of modern Ecuador and most of Peru; to the south was Collasuyu, the largest sector, which stretched eastward from the Pacific coast to beyond Lake Titicaca and southward about a third of the way down the coast of present-day Chile; Cuntisuyu extended westward; and, finally, Antisuyu, the smallest sector, opened eastward onto the Amazonian piedmont, which the Incas never really managed to subjugate, despite several attempts.

The Genius of the Incas Lay in the Political Organization of a Vast and Ethnically Heterogeneous Country

The immense expanse of territory under Inca domination may seem astounding, but it was in keeping with a long Andean tradition. At regular intervals through the centuries, brilliant all-conquering civilizations had arisen along the Andean Cordillera.

According to legend, there was a succession of twelve Inca emperors at Cuzco. Nowadays there is agreement that the ninth sovereign, Pachacuti (top), actually should be considered the first Inca. His name means "inversion of the world order." It was he who rebuilt the town of Cuzco and constructed the network of roads. He also promoted the cult of Viracocha, believed to be the Creator who had caused the sun to rise from Lake Titicaca. The Inca Huascar, Huayna Capac's son, is pictured above.

The number of Inca dynasties and their basis in historical reality are a matter of debate. The Incas believed that the emperor, or Great Inca, was himself the son of the sun, and they worshiped him accordingly: No lord or king, no matter how powerful, could approach the emperor without carrying a burden on his back, as a sign of humility. Paintings from the colonial period always represent Inca kings with their emblems: a "scepter," in the form of an ax, and a royal fringed headdress, or *mascapaicha*. This 17th-century painting shows two Inca emperors, Topa Yupanqui (left) and Lloque Yupanqui (right).

More than 2500 years ago, one such civilization—known as the Chavín culture—emerged in the central Andes (northern Peru) and extended its influence as far as the coast. In the 7th century AD, the Mochica developed another original culture—evidenced in splendid figurative ceramics—consolidating several disparate peoples in the valleys of the northern Andes. In the 10th century AD emerged two other cultures, centered around the cities of Tiwanaku, on the shore of Lake Titicaca, and Wari, situated to the northwest of Cuzco. Not long before the Incas came to power, the individual chiefdoms of Peru's northern coast had united to form one kingdom, called Chimor, based in the city of Chan Chan.

Meanwhile, in the south, there first arose (at about the same time as the Chavín culture in the north) the Paracas civilization, which produced fine painted pottery, rich woven textiles, and the seaside necropolises that had so deeply impressed Pizarro's men. Later, from about 600 BC until AD 500, there flourished along the coast of southern Peru what is perhaps the most well-known of all the pre-Inca civilizations: the Nazca. Famous for their colorful ceramics and textiles, the people of the Nazca culture are perhaps most renowned for having carved—or, more precisely, swept—into the land huge geometric and figural drawings. The interpretation of these drawings, known as geoglyphs, has stumped anthropologists even today, as they can truly be appreciated only from the sky.

It is truly an art to govern many often hostile ethnic groups, an art that rests on three principles: first, the centralization of power; second, an efficient bureaucracy to administer the conquered provinces; and finally, the use of one language throughout the entire territory. In the case of the Incas, the central power was personified by the Great Inca in the city of Cuzco; the bureaucratic system was staffed by *orejónes,* the Inca's ambassadors; and the Quechua language was imposed upon all the conquered cultures.

Unification was not always accomplished without a hitch, however. The last lord of Chimor, in particular, courageously resisted the Incas for some time—but in

According to tradition, the first Incas—four men and four women—emerged from a cave known as Pacaritambo. A fanciful Italian engraving of 1820 shows Manco Capac, one of the first four men, and Queen Mama Huaco, his sister and bride, accepting the submission of the natives.

vain. The natives that Pizarro met at Tumbes belonged to that powerful kingdom, and they had long resented Inca domination. The northern regions of the Ecuadorian Andes, conquered by the Inca with some difficulty at the beginning of the 16th century, also displayed hostility to the central power.

In order to secure dominion over these distant territories, the Inca resorted to a policy that proved effective in many instances. It consisted of moving entire populations so as to break up local solidarity. Hence, families from Cuzco or other "safe" provinces were transported thousands of miles and settled among

Because of the realism of its forms and depictions, Mochica pottery (examples above) enables us to reconstruct certain aspects of this culture, in which shamanism, human sacrifice, and ritual eroticism played an important role.

foreign peoples, for example, in the valleys near Quito or in those of Tucumán (now Argentina). Conversely, groups belonging to regional chiefdoms were moved into areas that were culturally attached to the Cuzco authorities.

Despite these practices, rebellion smoldered in many areas. Even as the Spaniards were sailing along the Pacific coast, a rebellion against the Inca's authority broke out in the region around Quito, which had only recently been conquered. Great Inca Huayna Capac went there in person and subdued the rebels with a cruelty that has stuck in local memory. After a battle at Otavalo, about forty miles northeast of Quito, the corpses of slaughtered rebels thrown into a lake turned its waters red; since then it has been called Yawar Cocha, the "lake of blood."

These images are very different from the peaceful picture of Inca expansion painted later by Cuzco authorities and repeated in Spanish accounts (for a long time our only source of information about the period, since the Incas kept no written records). In particular, the writings of Garcilaso de la Vega (c. 1535–1616), a chronicler of both Inca and Spanish descent, propagated widely the often unrealistic image of great and generous Inca lords full of wisdom.

Having pacified the surrounding territory, Huayna Capac reached Quito, the second city of the empire. There gloomy portents announced that a catastrophe was imminent: an earthquake of unusual violence, terrifying visions, and, finally, the messenger sent by the *oréjon* at Tumbes, who warned of the arrival by sea of white men.

Misfortune Arrived in the Form of an Unknown Disease— Smallpox

In 1526 Huayna Capac died of smallpox, without having met a single one of the foreigners who had brought this terrible sickness to his

In 1528, equipped with precise information and proof concerning the wealth of the mysterious El Dorado, Pizarro returned to Spain, where Charles V granted him the governorship of the vast territory to be conquered. Below is an engraving showing Pizarro at court.

empire. His embalmed corpse was carried to Cuzco, while a crisis began over his succession, pitting Huascar, a legitimate son, against Atahualpa, an illegitimate one. The former was named Inca at Cuzco, the latter was proclaimed sovereign at Quito. Thus, while the Spaniards were preparing for their conquest, civil strife between Quito and Cuzco shook the region.

In 1528 Pizarro returned to Spain to persuade the king to finance the conquest of Peru. It was a stroke of good luck for him that he was forced to postpone his enterprise: Five years later he was able to take advantage of the fratricidal war that was tearing the Inca empire apart and himself destroy the dynasty of the Incas.

Huascar, depicted in this 17th-century painting (above), was the legitimate heir to the Inca empire. Pizarro tried to ally himself with Huascar, but Atahualpa's supporters took Huascar prisoner and assassinated him to prevent such a collaboration.

By 1532 Pizarro had returned to Peru, this time for good. He had at his disposal sixty-three horsemen and two hundred infantrymen —a paltry number, but he believed in his luck and his own ability. At Tumbes he found no longer the lively port he had visited before, but a town ravaged by war and pestilence.

CHAPTER II
THE PASSION OF ATAHUALPA

An illustration from *Les Incas* (1777), by Jean-François Marmontel, showing Alonzo de Molina (the Spaniard who had remained at Tumbes when Pizarro returned to Panama) being offered a choice of beautiful brides by the Inca governor (opposite). On this page is a map of the port of Callao, Peru, at the time of the conquest.

Quickly fleeing these devastated regions, the conquistadors headed for Cajamarca, where they knew from local scouts that Atahualpa—one of the two warring brothers—was to be found. They followed a splendid paved highway, similar in construction to ancient Roman roads, that scaled the steepest slopes by turning into a staircase. The highway formed part of a vast road system, the creation of which was attributed to Huayna Capac's father and probably spanned several decades. Composed of two longitudinal axes (one following the coast, the other the crest of the mountain range) joined together by many lateral roads, this remarkable network allowed effective communication among the provinces, despite the formidable obstacles presented by the Andean mountain ranges. Messengers known as *chasquis* maintained interior connections, making all their journeys on foot and relieving each other every few miles. The service was so efficient that the Great Inca in the city of Cuzco was said to be able to eat fish that his *chasquis* brought him fresh from the seashore.

Reaching the city of Caxas, the conquistadors found a population exasperated by the cruelty of Atahualpa and complaining of the heavy tribute imposed by the Incas. Not only did the central power levy a large part of everything they produced, but it also demanded that children be sacrificed to it every year.

Inca engineering astonished the Spaniards. The walls of Sacsahuaman (left) are an outstanding example of Inca masonry, its huge irregular stones fitted together with minute precision.

"Pizarro set out, with the horse and foot, marching along the sea coast, which was well peopled, and placing all the villages under the dominion of his Majesty; for their lords, with one accord, came out into the roads to receive the Governor, without making any opposition. The Governor, far from doing them any harm or showing any anger, received them all lovingly, and they were taught some things touching our holy Catholic Faith by the monks who accompanied the expedition."

Francisco de Xeres
The Conquest of Peru
1534

Pizarro conquering Peru, an early 17th-century engraving (left).

Chosen from Among the Most Beautiful Children and Usually from the Most Powerful Families, the Future Victims Are Accorded Every Honor

The selected children traveled to Cuzco, where they were received by the Inca with great pomp. On returning to their villages, however, the children were entombed in caves or thrown down ravines. Their deaths, which were believed to keep suffering and illness from the Inca, also conferred great prestige on the victims' families. It sometimes happened that the community itself decided

Inca law was harsh, and clemency on the part of the rulers all the more gratefully received. In an early 19th-century artist's reconstruction, Mayta Capac pardons two malefactors.

EL TERZERO MES MARZO
PACHA PVCVY

Sacrificio con el Taraz negro

In the region of Lake Titicaca, the people sacrificed a black llama, an *urcu,* before setting off to war. At left is a drawing of this rite made by Felipe Guamán Poma de Ayala.

to sacrifice one of its children to secure general prosperity. Although these practices were forbidden in the first years of Spanish colonization, they continued sporadically until the start of the 20th century.

Far more common were animal sacrifices, which also had to follow certain rules: The animals' coats had to be plain and their fur silky, for example. According to some chroniclers, in the city of Cuzco more than ten thousand llamas were sometimes killed in the course of a single ceremony. While probably exaggerated, this figure nevertheless gives an indication of the scale of the rites.

In Caxas the Spaniards also noticed three corpses hanging by the feet. When they asked the reason for this punishment, they were told that these men had dared enter the house of the *aclla,* the women sworn to the Inca's service. Chosen from among the most beautiful girls of each ethnic group and, as young girls, separated from the communities of their birth and cloistered for life, the *aclla,* "virgins of the sun," could neither marry nor have sexual relations without the sovereign's permission. Anyone who dared to cross the threshold of their residence was condemned to death, and their families disgraced. In the house reserved for them, the *aclla* devoted themselves to weaving and sewing the Inca's clothes.

Indeed, weaving was one of the key elements of Inca civilization, and Pizarro and his men, recognizing that it was the basis of all trade, eagerly offered shirts from the Spanish region of Castile to the inhabitants of Caxas. Amazed by the quality of the Andean fabrics, the Spaniards very quickly learned to distinguish the *ahuasca,* worn by the common people, from the precious *cumbi,* the privilege of the elite, who shunned alpaca and llama wool in favor of the soft fleece of the vicuña.

Chosen from each community for their beauty, the *aclla* were given to the Inca as a sign of allegiance. He could then redistribute these women to the nobles as a reward for their services.

"The Sin of Cora the Priestess"

In Jean-François Marmontel's novel *Les Incas* (1777), Alonzo de Molina falls in love with Cora, a priestess of the sun, and she with him. By a fortunate chance he is able to rescue her from her convent during a volcanic eruption. They wander in the fields and enjoy a brief idyll of happiness before Cora, in fear, returns to her temple. Although fictitious, the story reflects historical reality. The virgins of the sun renounced normal relationships and prepared food and drink for their "husband," the sun. Consecrated at the age of twelve in a cycle of ceremonies, they then underwent a kind of novitiate that lasted three years, at the end of which the high priest invited them to make a definitive choice between marriage and consecration to the sun as an *aclla*.

The Inca's Law

If a woman consecrated to the sun betrayed her vows by falling in love with a mortal and losing her virginity, she was buried alive and her lover was hanged. If the man was already married, the Inca also ordered the man's wife, children, and entire family to be killed, as well as all members of his community and their animals. The houses of his village were razed, and the earth sprinkled with salt so that nothing would grow and the accursed place could serve as a warning to everyone. (In Marmontel's novel, Cora and her family nearly meet this fate, but Alonzo steps forward, takes the blame upon himself, and persuades the Inca to abolish the priestesses' vow of celibacy.) Isabel Yarucpalla, one of Atahualpa's wives, was given to the conquistador Juan Lobato de Sosa. She adopted the Spanish way of life and even thwarted a plot by Inca officials in Quito to massacre the Spanish.

The Conquistadors Understood That in Andean Societies Weaving Had a Far More Important Function Than the Strictly Utilitarian

The Inca used the luxurious *cumbi* wool to demonstrate his generosity when he appointed his associates. If a lord swore him allegiance, the ruler rewarded the noble by offering him *cumbi* and thus secured his loyalty. One chronicler reports that when the conflict over the succession broke out, Atahualpa sent Huascar some fabrics of extreme beauty. The latter, furious, threw them on the fire, crying, "Does he think that we do not have equally beautiful ones here, or is he just trying to hide his treason with this gift?"

Pizarro, who was just beginning to learn about Andean customs, had not yet grasped the significance of these fabrics. But a few years later his compatriots had some of the designs interpreted by native informants and learned that they constituted a form of writing. According to some testimonies, the Incas recorded the history of the dynasties on the embroideries (*quellca*). Indeed, the word *quellca* was used in the colonial period to mean writing. The finest *quellca* were sent, in 1570, to King Philip II of Spain to decorate the walls of the royal palace in Madrid. Unfortunately, all trace of these fabrics has disappeared, and the mystery of their meaning remains unsolved.

Textile workshops (such as the ones depicted in these 17th-century drawings, above) were founded by the Spaniards on the basis of the Incas' ancestral knowledge of weaving. Soon after the conquest, they were to become true capitalist enterprises staffed by a native workforce. The products that were manufactured were made for local markets, which enabled them to avoid the taxes levied on European merchandise. Despite the deplorable working conditions, the workshops were extremely successful, especially those in the northern Andes.

Trophy heads such as the ones shown on these Paracas textiles (left, above and below) are a common motif in the iconography of the coastal civilizations and recall the human head-hunting practiced by Amazonian peoples. The Incas did not practice decapitation. Instead, defeated enemies were massacred, the chiefs flayed, and their stretched skin used to make drums.

A braided wool ornament in the form of a figure (above).

Leaving Caxas, Pizarro set out toward Cajamarca across frozen tundra. In places the men reached altitudes of over 13,000 feet, where the cold was intense and even the horses became ill. The Spaniards were astonished to encounter pyramidal stone fortresses and storehouses filled with fabrics and food, enough to meet a conquering Inca army's needs for several weeks. Crossing the rivers they found another cause for astonishment: Whereas in the valleys river crossings were made by raft, the mountain torrents were crossed using rope bridges or baskets suspended from cables. Moreover, all these crossing points were supervised, and nobody could carry a load across without paying a toll.

The Incas built several types of bridges: slabs resting on stone pillars, called *rumichacas;* simple tree trunks; and suspension bridges made from lianas and plaited agave fibers—like that near Penipé (left above) or the one that still hangs over the Apurimac River. Alternatively, the traveler could use an *oroya,* a kind of basket in which he or she could slide along a cable (opposite). A *chaca suyuyoc,* or "governor of the bridges," was in charge of all these civil engineering works.

The fortress of Ingapirca (left), famous for its circular shape, was built at the time of the Spanish conquest in the region of the Cañari, a people who lived to the south of present-day Ecuador.

The Use of the Bridges and the Road Network Was Subject to Very Strict Controls

Thus, even before reaching Cajamarca, the Spaniards learned that they were dealing with a highly controlled culture very different from the confusion that reigned in the northern chiefdoms. Arriving in the town where Atahualpa had established his headquarters, the conquistadors soon realized that their only resource against this powerfully organized civilization was cunning. It did not take long for the fear inspired by the Spaniards' horses and the arquebuses to die down, nor for the Incas to become aware that the white men were not invulnerable. It was clear that Atahualpa intended to exploit the foreigners, or at least to use them against Huascar. The tension began to mount beneath the sun of Cajamarca.

This town impressed the Spaniards even more than Caxas. Its central square, bigger than the largest square in Spain, was bordered by beautifully proportioned buildings of fitted stone, whose construction displayed remarkable architectural techniques. One superb building devoted to the cult of the sun stood at the town entrance.

The Spaniards and the Inca began negotiations that would lead to a meeting of the foreigners and the would-be emperor: First, a messenger explained to the strangers that Atahualpa was fasting. Envoys were then exchanged, and each side watched the other. Finally, Pizarro sent his brother, Hernando, to Atahualpa.

An 18th-century version of the costumes of an Inca and his wife (below left). Opposite: Inca princes and a princess; the first figure is in Spanish costume, the other two in traditional dress.

The Conquistador Found the Inca Seated on a Low Chair, Surrounded by Numerous Dignitaries and a Few of His Women, Including His Own Sister

The sovereign, whom Hernando guessed was about thirty years old, was dressed in the most delicate fabrics and crowned with the royal insignia—a woolen braid that was wound five times around the head, partially covering the forehead, and from which there hung a fringe of red wool interwoven with gold. His earlobes were fitted with a gold disks. Atahualpa's face was hidden by a very fine veil: As the son of the sun, his person was too powerful to be seen by human eyes. The Spaniards demanded that the sovereign remove the veil. He did so, although without bestowing a single glance on them. He then exhorted them to return all the woven fabrics they had stolen en route. After this somewhat frosty conversation, Atahualpa agreed to meet Pizarro in Cajamarca's central square. Next

TEMPLE DU SOLEIL.

The solar cult was imposed throughout the empire in addition to many local cults. The most important event in the religious calendar was the festival of the sun, or Inti Rami, celebrated at the summer solstice. On this occasion, the lords would come to Cuzco to deliver tribute to the Great Inca, who in return gave them gifts of cloth, *aclla,* and other prestigious goods. The Incas also went to the temple of Vilcañota (one of the most important in the empire), a pilgrimage meant to relive the mythical journey of the first Inca, Manco Capac, and his wife, Mama Huaco. Here, children from every province were sacrificed to the sun.

Left: A 19th-century engraving of an Inca sun temple.

Atahualpa offered the Spaniards some maize beer served in large golden goblets. The conquistadors at first refused, but they ultimately gave way to the Inca's threatening insistence. It was the custom: In order to open negotiations, the more powerful party offered a drink. This could not be refused without causing offense.

The decisive meeting between the two sides took place the following day. Pizarro had ordered his men to hide, but to be ready to intervene if he called out the name of Saint James. The arrival of the Inca was an extraordinary spectacle. He was carried in a litter lavishly decorated with parrot feathers, and bodyguards covered in sheets of gold and dressed in the richest costumes surrounded him. The imperial procession was preceded by a troop of youngsters who swept the ground before the Inca with meticulous care. A colorfully dressed crowd escorted the procession to the sound of conch shells and flutes.

Atahualpa's meeting with Pizarro in the Cajamarca square was a turning point in South American history. This engraving, made soon after the event, shows Atahualpa being borne on a litter by his lords (below).

ATHABALIBA

The title of Inca was hereditary, but the sovereign could choose the son who was best suited to succeed him. Royal incest—the model for which was the mythical couple of Manco Capac and Mama Huaco—preserved the dynasty's endogamous reproduction, while polygamy enabled the sovereign to forge solid alliances with the regional nobility. Atahualpa (left) is said to have had more than five thousand concubines.

Among the goods that the Incas received as tribute from the tribes of the Amazonian piedmont, gold and feathers of rare birds—especially of macaws living in the Amazonian forest—were considered the most precious. This Chancay textile is made of both feathers and gold.

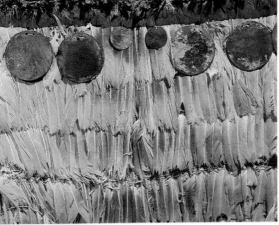

Under Their Brightly Colored Clothes, the Cajamarcans Hid Slings and Clubs

Each adult male was obligated to provide his services, or "tribute," to the Inca, the principal nobles of his region, and his own community.

In less than an hour, the destiny of the empire was completely overturned. On Pizarro's orders, Vicente de Valverde, a Dominican priest, advanced toward the Inca brandishing a cross in one hand and a Bible or breviary in the other. "I have come to teach you the words of God," he said. Atahualpa seized the book, put it to his ear, and threw it violently to the ground. This impious gesture unleashed Pizarro's anger. He grabbed the arm of the son of the sun, whom nobody was supposed to touch, and tried to throw him down from the litter. A terrible confusion followed, punctuated by arquebus shots and the neighing of horses. When calm was restored, the square was strewn with bodies. All that was left were a few terrorized natives and a dishonored emperor, his clothes torn and his hands tied.

Atahualpa, in an attempt to save his own life, proposed to Pizarro that he would fill a room of his dwelling with all the treasures of his kingdom. This would be the price of his ransom. Soon from the coast, the mountains, and the four corners of the land flowed numerous loads of precious objects. Atahualpa, imprisoned, struck up a friendship with Hernando, Pizarro's brother, while he waited for the ransom to be collected. Together they played interminable games of dice. The Inca, in his gilded prison, was allowed to keep his women and his clothes, including a magnificent cape

of bat hair much admired by his guards. The ransom accumulated, and Pizarro reserved a fifth of it for the king of Spain. Having set aside the king's and his own share of the booty, Pizarro divided the rest among his men. Never had soldiers become so rich so quickly. And never were such fortunes squandered so rapidly, all too often at a throw of the dice.

Above: A Chimú knife with a gold figured handle. The Spaniards melted the golden vases and objects of Atahualpa's ransom into ingots, and today very little Inca gold survives. It has been calculated that there were more than six tons of gold and more than twelve tons of silver. Silver was so abundant that the Spaniards used it to shoe their horses.

Left: Atahualpa promising to fill the room with gold as ransom for his life.

The Death of Atahualpa

It was while Hernando, Atahualpa's only friend, was absent that the drama came to its climax. Alarming news reached Pizarro from Quito. Some generals faithful to Atahualpa had assassinated Huascar, having suspected him of collaboration with the Spaniards. One of Atahualpa's generals was threatening to come to Cajamarca to liberate his lord. Whether Pizarro feared a rebellion or used these rumors as a pretext to break his promise, the fact remains that he accused Atahualpa of high treason and condemned him to be burned at the stake. One cannot imagine a more cruel sentence: The Incas had an absolute terror of cremation because it caused the body to disappear. So Atahualpa agreed to

Before surrendering to the executioner, Atahualpa begged Pizarro to take care of his children. His corpse remained on show in the square throughout the night, and the following day it was carried into the church of San Francisco. It is said that his loyal subjects secretly exhumed the body and transported the Inca's remains to Quito. Below: A 19th-century print showing Atahualpa's funeral.

convert to Catholicism on the condition that he have his head cut off instead. (Atahualpa swore that, if decapitated, he would return one day to avenge his people, and even today, in the mountains of Peru, myths circulate that promise the impending return of Inkarri, a kind of messiah whose head will sprout from beneath the earth.)

On the day of Atahualpa's execution, the sky became dark. Some of his wives and his sister hanged themselves to accompany him and serve him in the afterlife, a very widespread custom in the northern Andes on the death of a great lord. Pizarro hastened to enthrone one of Atahualpa's younger brothers, a weak and easily manipulated character, as Inca. But this child died of poison some time afterward. At Pizarro's wish once

For the Romantic writers and artists of the 19th century, the Inca civilization became a sort of Golden Age, imagined as a society of peace and harmony, a vision that was far from reality. Above: A section of panoramic wallpaper manufactured in 1826.

again, another of the Inca's brothers, Manco, took his place and became sovereign.

Pedro, Pizarro's cousin, gives an entirely different version of Atahualpa's end. According to him, the emperor's death was plotted by Felipillo, the young interpreter from Tumbes whom the Spaniards had taken along during their first coastal voyage. Felipillo had good reason to hate the Inca, for his community of Chimor had been forced to capitulate to Atahualpa's predecessor, Huayna Capac. Moreover, during Atahualpa's captivity, the boy had fallen in love with one of the Inca's wives and had conceived the idea of betraying him. He is said to have produced a deliberately false translation of some crucial information, which caused a misunderstanding that cost the fallen emperor his life.

Topa Amaru (opposite), the last Inca, was defeated and executed by Spaniards in 1572, his head displayed on the end of a pike. During his lifetime he had been renowned for his beauty. According to legend, the head became more beautiful every day, and the Inca's supporters came by night to worship it in secret. In order to put an end to this cult, the Spanish viceroy had it buried.

Atahualpa's Death Sealed the Fate of the Empire of the Four Quarters. In 1533 the Spaniards Entered the City of Cuzco and Pillaged the Temple of the Sun

But the colonial administration had to endure some troubled years at the start. There were problems on two fronts. On the one hand, the Spaniards began to quarrel among themselves, forming two factions—one led by Pizarro, the other by his erstwhile companion, Almagro. On the other hand, the natives still refused to submit to the conquistadors. After being cruelly humiliated by the Spaniards, the puppet sovereign, Manco, fled with his army to outposts high in the Andes (the legendary fortresses of Vitcos and Vilcabamba), from which he organized the native resistance.

Manco's sons Titu Cusi and Topa Amaru would continue the struggle until 1572, when the latter was captured by the Spaniards and beheaded, just as his uncle Atahualpa had been forty years earlier. For the next three hundred years, Spanish law was to reign supreme in the Andean Cordilleras.

The principal Spanish leaders died feuding among themselves. Pizarro was assassinated in his palace in Lima on 26 July 1541.

TRAVAXOS
PAPAALLAIMITAPA

cha junio haucay cusqui quilla

labrador
pachaca

Once the Inca empire was overthrown, the conquistadors established the *encomienda,* an institution that was to prove catastrophic for the region's social and economic order and which began by unleashing bloody conflicts between the colonists and the representatives of the Spanish crown.

CHAPTER III
EVERYDAY LIFE AND WORK

Under Spanish rule, the natives were obliged to work harder than before for less reward. Their agricultural methods are depicted here in a late-16th-century illustration by Felipe Guamán Poma de Ayala (opposite). At right is depicted a battle between members of two Spanish factions.

In 1542 Charles V established the viceroyalty of Peru—
which then included all of Spanish South America and
Panama—and granted the conquistadors the right to
levy tribute from the conquered natives. In return, each
Spanish agent, or *encomendero,* undertook to protect
and convert to Christianity those placed under his
authority. This was known as the *encomienda* system. It
was similar to feudalism in that it was founded on ties
of dependence rather than actual ownership of a domain.

But the Spanish king soon began to disapprove of the
powerful factions forming in the Americas, as he was
able to exert very little control over them. So, under the
pretext of putting an end to the widespread abuses being
committed there (of which he kept himself well
informed), he decided to change the system and revoked
the perpetuity of the privilege. This measure provoked a
crisis. The conquistadors refused to yield and rebelled
against Charles V's representatives.

It Was only After Many Murderous Struggles That Royal Authority Finally Was Asserted

It was decreed that the properties, or *encomiendas,*
would remain in the
conquerors' hands until
the second generation,
when they would revert
to their "natural" owner,
the king. This
arrangement was not
always respected,
however, and some
encomiendas endured
until the 18th century.
The *encomenderos*
used their privileges
to increase their
political influence
and to
misappropriate
native labor for
their own profit.
The natives

The oppression of
the native peoples
by the Spanish privileged
class, which began with
the conquest, was to
last for three hundred
years. Here, in an
engraving of 1532, men
are being forced to carry
away plunder for their
Spanish masters.

tirelessly denounced these machinations before the courts. (Strange as it may sound, all the natives conquered by the Spaniards were considered vassals of the king of Spain and, as such, were protected by specific legislation.)

Forty Years After the Events in Cajamarca, the Situation Had Deteriorated Dramatically

Wars and epidemics caused a major demographic collapse, and the *encomienda* system broke up the traditional organization of the rural peasant communities. Many natives fled to escape the forced labor imposed on them by the Spaniards and sought refuge in the towns.

Philip II (a portrait by Titian, above) continued the politics of centralization established by his predecessor, Charles V, who had created the viceroyalty of Peru in 1542. An alter ego of the monarch, the viceroy was governor, chief of the armies, and president of the courts of justice. Around him was organized a court that reproduced, on a more modest scale, the pomp of that in Spain. His power was based on a bureaucratic system that divided up the territory. The important administrative posts were occupied by the viceroy's relatives—nepotism and corruption being an inherent part of the colonial system.

In order to put an end to the hemorrhage of the workforce that was undermining the economic foundations of the colonial system, Francisco de Toledo (1515–84), who had been made viceroy of Peru in 1569, conceived extensive administrative reforms based on territorial reorganization. In the accessible areas, villages were created and the indigenous populations redistributed among them. These agglomerations were laid out in a checkerboard arrangement around a central square bordered by the official buildings and the church. Such rearrangements, which merged ethnic groups (or were used, where necessary, to disperse the members of a single ethnic group), would gradually become parishes, each under the protection of a patron saint.

From the second half of the 16th century onward, Spanish officials traveled through the Cordilleras compiling a census of inhabitants and resources. Their task was easy, since the natives had always kept extremely precise records of agriculture, demography, and tribute. The foreigners merely had to obtain from the mouths of the local dignitaries—the *quipucamayoc* ("keepers of the *quipu*")—the information that the latter had recorded by means of knotted strings. Known as *quipu,* the strings

The village of Palca (top), with a traditional-style church surrounded by a wall. Native porters were made to carry Spanish travelers on their backs (above).

constituted an information storage system that denoted and enumerated different classes of people, plants, or objects. Although the language of these *quipu* has not been fully deciphered, we know that they also recorded nonquantitative information, such as songs or dynastic tales.

Inca Society Was Based on Agriculture, and the Inca Ritually Took Part in the Great Labor of Sowing and Harvesting

It was the Great Inca himself who inaugurated with special rites the seasonal cycle of maize, a cycle

Knotted strings, or *quipu*, continued to be used as accounting devices after the conquest. The size of the knots and the colors used made it possible to record quantities with extreme precision (measures of coca, maize, or other agricultural products, numbers of tributaries, and debts that the *encomenderos* had imposed upon them). There were even "historical" *quipu* that recorded the most outstanding episodes of the Inca dynasties. This drawing of a *quipucamayoc* is by Felipe Guamán Poma de Ayala.

CŌTADOR·MAIOR·ITEZORERO
TAVANTINSVIO·QVIPO
CVRACA·CON DOR·CHAVA

punctuated by ceremonies aimed at increasing the fecundity of both humans and plants. An enormous expenditure of labor and a highly sophisticated management system were demanded by a territory that was poorly situated for agricultural exploitation. Sparse and stony soil, very steep slopes, difficult irrigation—the Incas succeeded in overcoming all these handicaps by building terraces and canals, many of which are still in use today. To bring water to arid land, they altered the course of rivers and bored through rock—an amazing technical feat considering they lacked iron tools. In fact, these techniques were used by pre-Inca civilizations, but the state organization of the sovereigns of Cuzco made it possible to work on a much grander scale than had been hitherto possible.

The most important agricultural tool used by the natives was a wooden spade, known as the *taclla*. Andean farmers were not familiar with the plow, and neither draft oxen nor the ard (a simple plow for turning over the earth)—both introduced by the Spaniards in the 16th century—would completely replace the old methods, at least not in the poorest areas.

Under the Inca administration agriculture was based chiefly on maize, quinoa, coca, and tubers (which include potatoes and oca). Potatoes grow well at high altitudes, even above 13,000

The sacred valley of the Incas follows the middle section of the Urubamba River, a few miles from Cuzco. At Pisac (opposite), the stepped terraces traversed the slopes for several hundred yards and produced the finest maize in the empire, especially destined for the lords' rituals. The whole valley belonged to the Inca and the royal family.

A peasant digging the ground with the peculiarly shaped Peruvian spade (below).

feet, and, without this staple, the Andean plateau could never have been populated by humans. In the region of Lake Titicaca, where the potato originated, dozens of varieties have been recorded. Thanks to the area's special climatic conditions, the potatoes could be preserved for the lean months of the year. The sharp variation between the nightly frosts and the tropical sun effected a process of dehydration that turned the potatoes into a substance known as *chuño*. This is still the staple food of many of the populations living at the higher altitudes. And the introduction of potatoes to Europe by the Spanish colonists enabled peasants there to overcome famine.

Maize, Which Grew in the Relatively Warm Valleys, Was More Than a Mere Food: Endowed with Ritual and Symbolic Value, It Was Offered to the Ancestors and to the Divinities of the Earth and the Cosmos

According to Inca mythology, Mama Huaco, sister and wife of the first Inca, was responsible for the origin of maize. She is said to have brought ears of corn out of the cave of Pacaritambo, the legendary place from which the eight founding Incas were said to have emerged. (For this reason, maize was also called "cave seeds.") The myth survives in southern Ecuador, where some still believe that the goddess they call Mamahuaca, mistress of the mountains and announcer of harvests, hides in a cave with a basket of golden ears of corn.

Coca had been cultivated for a very long time in the warm and rainy regions. During the reign of the

Chewing dried coca leaves was a practice so widespread among the natives that they always carried a little bag of woven wool, such as the one shown below, to hold a supply of the herbal stimulant.

Ancient Peruvian farming was geared for the production of both food and luxury goods. In this 17th-century watercolor (opposite) the most prominent features are macaws, used to make feather garments, and maize, the staple food. Left: A llama and a vicuña, both raised for their beautiful wool.

1 le Lama 2 la Vigogne

VUE DE LA CO

Cotopaxi
Volcan

Antisana *Me Neig* — Tongouragua *Volcan* — Quelendané — Guamani

LIGNE *Horizontale* — DU Bas *constant* — De — Sig do

LIGNE DE NIVEAU D

Incas, members of the elite had the right to chew it, a privilege accorded to the common people only in exceptional circumstances. The abolition of such restrictions at the end of the empire led to extensive consumption of the plant because coca, a stimulant, can keep both hunger and fatigue at bay. Trade in the crop soon burgeoned and very quickly made a fortune for the Spaniards. Like maize, coca also had a sacred nature: It was used as a devotional offering and as an instrument of divination—sorcerers and healers read the future in the patterns made by the leaves when they were thrown on the ground at random.

Apart from these crops, the Incas also raised herds of vicuñas and llamas, especially around Lake Titicaca. These animals were valued principally for their precious wool. Even when they were used as beasts of burden, they carried only light loads; heavier weights were transported on the backs of human porters.

Before the Spaniards arrived, the land was cultivated collectively. Families helped each other according to very strict rules of reciprocity, and at sowing and harvest time big gatherings were held during which maize beer (known as *chicha*) flowed like water. The Spaniards very quickly grew to be wary of these libations,

The volcanoes of the northern Cordillera were considered to be the abodes of supernatural beings who unleashed lightning and thunder. These deities formed couples and could take on human shape. The lakes that formed in the craters were also thought to be inhabited by these divinities, to whom peasants brought offerings of plants or human sacrifices.

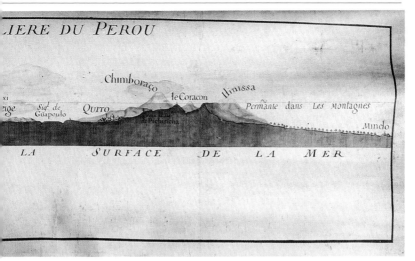

...IERE DU PEROU

Chimboraço   leCoraçon   Ilinissa

xi   Siat de   QUITO   Permãnte dans Les Montagnes
...que   Guapoulo

   Pichincha   Mindo

LA   SURFACE   DE   LA   MER

which sparked off quarrels and engendered a strong sense of solidarity among the natives.

In the Cordilleras, High Altitudes and Tropical or Equatorial Latitudes Create a Series of Different Geographical Zones, One Above the Other

In Ecuador, for example, very dense forest covers the slopes between 9000 and 10,000 feet. In ancient Peru and Bolivia, the zone above 10,000 feet was considered to be the most appropriate for permanent habitation. It was here that the Incas built their villages, close to the maize fields. Above 13,000 feet stretched the cold heathlands of the *puna,* which were devoted to pasture and the cultivation of tubers. Finally, below 6500 feet the people of the Andes tended their coca and cotton plantations.

The ideal, for native communities, was to be able to exploit all three ecological levels, for in this way they could have access to all the necessary resources. Since these zones were sometimes quite far apart, the communities would send entire families—*mitimaes*—to the lowlands and highlands to spend a few months cultivating

The flowers and fruits of the New World fascinated European botanists, but were only slowly catalogued. This detail (below) comes from a book published in 1802.

there. (The term *mitimaes* referred to any displaced population, as well as the military garrisons installed by the Inca in annexed territories.) The originality of this system of land use lay not only in the permanent establishment of agricultural colonies detached from the nucleus of the home village, but also in the exploitation of a single zone by several different ethnic groups, originating from several centers.

This concept of territory contrasts markedly with that of the Europeans—for whom an agricultural domain is almost always in a single, proprietary block—and shows that ethnic barriers do not constitute an impediment to the collective utilization of a single zone.

In Peru the Conquest Was Characterized By the Exchange of Plants, Animals, and Techniques of Domestication

The Spaniards studied native plants and began to incorporate them in their daily diet and to use them for medicinal purposes. Conversely, the domestic animals imported to Peru by the conquerors—cows, horses, mules, pigs, chickens, goats, and sheep—transformed the ecological balance, dietary practices, and social relationships of the Andean world. The horse, forbidden to commoners, could only be ridden by descendants of the Inca nobility, and thus became a symbol of social superiority. Sheep soon displaced llamas, and pigs and cattle damaged many of the cereal fields, despite the fact that the Spaniards banned pastures on the edge of communal lands.

Sea conches such as this one (above) were used as trumpets, their solemn sound marking the rhythms of communal work and religious ceremony. Considered to be precious objects, they also served as offerings.

Every four years, a vicuña and deer hunt took place on the high plateaus, as depicted in this 17th-century illustration (left). The Inca himself took an active part in these hunts, which involved thousands of people.

Like other great civilizations, Inca Peru was based primarily on the tribute paid by the peasantry. The *quipucamayoc* took care of the accounts, and officials, called *caciques,* kept a watchful eye on the work being done. The *cacique,* who was placed at the head of a community comprised of a group of domestic units (*ayllu*), redistributed the land every year according to the number of active people in each household. These pre-Inca customs underwent a preliminary reorganization in Inca times, when the land at the disposal of each *ayllu* was divided into three unequal parts: The largest

The Spaniards imported into Peru huge numbers of domestic animals previously unknown there, such as horses, donkeys, cows, oxen, mules, dogs, sheep, goats, rabbits, and pigs. These animals proliferated with great speed, and some—for instance rabbits and pigs—became wild again and provided the indigenous communities with a new subsistence activity: hunting. The techniques of hunting large game were more or less the same in all the Andean regions. The men formed vast circles that covered the entire terrain. By moving toward the circle's center they surrounded the animals, which were then felled with pikes and clubs. The meat was dried and thus could be preserved for several months.

was given to the community to farm, while the other two were consecrated to the cult of the sun and to the state, respectively. The communities also paid a tribute of textiles (which were stockpiled in state depots), and they were periodically subject to a labor tax, known as *mita* service, levied during the construction of all collective works, including highways, monuments, and irrigation canals.

For administrative purposes, the different provinces comprising the empire of the Four Quarters were subdivided into complex tributary systems, which fitted into each other rather like Russian dolls. All able-bodied men from eighteen to fifty years of age were required to pay tribute in one form or another.

Cut into the hardest granite, the canals built by the Incas constitute one of that civilization's miracles of engineering.

The Collectivization of Work Gave Considerable Advantage to the Heads of Large Families

Four *waranga,* each comprising a group of one thousand tributaries, constituted an important economic unit and were presided over by a delegate from the city of Cuzco, quite frequently a member of the imperial family. The principle of division into four went beyond the framework of simple quantification, for it expressed a very subtle symbolic conception of space.

The Incas rigorously controlled the social categories that determined who was to pay tribute. Marriage, the primary condition for becoming a fully fledged tributary, was a matter of state, and could be contracted only with the consent of the sovereign or his representative. A man of high rank could wed several women (one of whom was considered the principal wife),

and these would share a communal residence. Such polygamy provided the tributary both with a workforce for the production of fabrics and, even more important, numerous progeny.

It is noteworthy that the Quechua language has more than four hundred expressions for describing human activities. This exaltation of labor—and the native tradition of tribute—partially explains the ease with which the natives submitted to the new rules for paying tribute to the Spaniards, even if they all complained to the representatives of the viceroy Francisco de Toledo about the increased burden of labor that weighed them down and threatened their own crops.

Thus, the Spaniards Found an Elaborate System of Tribute and a Work Discipline That They Could Easily Abuse

In 1545 the Spaniards discovered the mines of Mount Potosí in Bolivia, thanks to information provided by a

Kinship played an important role in the organization of social groups. Dictionaries of the Quechua language written by Spanish missionaries in the 16th and 17th centuries went into great detail about the terminology of kinship in an attempt to define degrees of blood ties. For instance, the same term designated a great-grandfather and a great-grandson, indicating the cyclical nature of the Inca concept of time. Below is shown an Inca wedding, in a colored engraving of 1820.

local laborer. The Spaniards immediately began to exploit the mines intensively, and by the second half of the 16th century huge quantities of silver were flowing to Europe on a regular basis.

Mount Potosí, which was bursting with so much silver that it appeared inexhaustible, was transformed into a truly awful place: Tunnels were dug at an altitude of about 16,000 feet, creating gaping mouths in the iridescent slopes that looked as if they wanted to swallow up the ghostly landscape.

The *minero,* the person who found a seam, could either work it directly or lease it out, though on the condition that one-fifth of the profits were reserved for the Spanish crown. What else but poverty and the lure of gain could explain the extraordinary expansion that this place was to undergo during the colonial period? Adventurers, people at odds with their communities, merchants, the nouveau riche, the lords who had joined the bourgeoisie, financiers, cooks, and prostitutes would turn this sinister region into a living urban center, endowed with twenty-five churches and strongly linked to the economic expansion of the West.

In Theory, Anybody Could Become a *Minero,* But in Reality, Working a Seam Was Too Costly for the Natives

The actual working of a mine was carried out partly by forced labor and partly by "free" workers who were paid in kind, not in money. There was no salaried class to speak of. The freedom of these miners, however, was quite relative: In order to meet their basic needs, the majority of them became indebted, usually for life, to the owner of the seam.

The working conditions in these tunnels were inhuman.

Most Inca gold was procured by panning rather than mining. Stone dams were built across rivers, and gold particles were collected from the stones, as shown in this Colombian engraving (above).

Forced to work without a break, some miners died of exhaustion underground before they could reach fresh air. Some seams were accessible only to children, who were made to crawl through cracks in the rock. Parents sometimes preferred to deform a child's legs at birth, since lameness would exempt them from this appalling but obligatory service.

If the exploitation of these sites was profitable and enabled the Spaniards to accumulate substantial fortunes for more than two hundred years, it was due not so much to the quality of the mineral as to the existence of an abundant, cheap workforce that was subjected to hideously ruthless oppression.

When the Spaniards discovered the rich veins of silver at Mount Potosí in Bolivia (below), they tapped this source in a way that had never been attempted under the Incas, using the natives as slave laborers. The shrine at the top of the mountain held one of the most famous statues of the Virgin in the empire.

Using repression one moment and persuasion the next, the 17th-century Spaniards were bent on destroying the rites and beliefs of the native peoples. By cutting them off from their ancestral roots, the conquerors brought about an irreparable break with Inca customs and traditions.

CHAPTER IV
THE ERADICATION OF IDOLATRY

To convert the natives to Christianity was one of the major objectives of the conquest, undertaken in large measure by Franciscan friars (pictured opposite). Peruvian ideas of Christianity, however, retained a strange ambivalence. Archangels were imagined as armed Spanish grandees with wings (right).

A lawyer by training, Spaniard Polo de Ondegardo arrived in the Andes in the mid 16th century, a time when the entire region was still troubled by the revolt of the *encomenderos*. Appointed *corregidor* (magistrate) first of Cuzco and then of Potosí, two towns of primary importance to the government of the viceroyship, Polo de Ondegardo was to play a key role in the campaign against native religious practices.

The Spaniards knew that the Incas venerated the remains of their ancestors. Dressed in fine fabrics, covered in jewels, and surrounded by precious objects, these mummies had aroused the greed of the conquistadors, who unhesitatingly violated numerous tombs to steal the treasures they contained.

The Incas believed that the life force of humans did not disappear at their death, but that these spiritual beings gathered in the beyond, eating and drinking as if they were alive. Mummies of the pre-Inca Paracas culture (above) were wrapped in beautiful woven textiles (left). Below is a feather headdress on a skull from the Nazca culture. Opposite: A pre-Inca cemetery on the coast near Lima.

Polo de Ondegardo was a politician, not an adventurer. By questioning the native nobles of Cuzco and probably making them promises of which we know nothing, he discovered the places where the Incas' mummies were hidden. He then had them removed from their funerary dwellings and destroyed by fire. Because the cult of the dead was of enormous importance in Andean societies, this act had serious consequences. The benevolence of the ancestors was believed necessary for a good harvest, and the corpses delivered messages to the living, through an interpreter; the bodies of the ancients, and anything that touched them, also possessed therapeutic qualities.

False heads were placed on top of the funerary bundles in which the body was wrapped to give them human form. On some of these faces the eyes are represented by shells and the nose by a triangular piece of wood. Often the head wears a wig of plant fibers topped by a bonnet or turban.

Only Incas and Members of the Nobility Had the Privilege of Being Embalmed and Were Invested with the Gift of Clairvoyance

Their internal organs were buried in receptacles, and their corpses were filled with tar and then dried by the same method used for preserving potatoes and meat: that is, exposed alternatingly to night frosts and the severity of the sun. The mummies, curled up in the fetal position, were not buried but placed in natural cavities, niches, or caves.

During the important festivities linked to the agricultural calendar or the celebration of military victories, the mummies of the Incas were taken from their resting places and transported with great pomp into the temple of the sun at Cuzco or onto the main square. Dressed in sumptuous garments and seated on golden chairs as befitted their rank, they were placed side by side with the principal divinities. They were given food and drink, and people danced before them. This cult of the ancestors was onerous not only because land had to be set aside in order to provide food for these mummies, but because a considerable workforce was compelled to take turns working in these fields.

Indeed, in the final years of his reign, the Inca Huascar, stepbrother and enemy of Atahualpa, wanted to suppress the cult of the mummies, which was far too costly a

burden to bear. But this aroused the hostility of the noble families and may be what brought him an ignominious death: He perished by drowning in the Andamarca River, and was hence deprived of immortality.

In the early years of the conquest, the Spaniards tried in vain to make Christian burial obligatory. But the natives, believing the deceased would suffer from the weight of the earth, secretly exhumed their dead and took them back to their funerary niches. Little by little, however, the priests succeeded in instilling in their wards a fear of the next world and of ghosts, wandering souls without graves who would take revenge on the living by sending them illnesses. So the Catholic funerary rite finally won, but Andean peasants have retained the custom, after the death of a relative or a neighbor, of washing themselves in a river along with all the deceased's possessions, to protect themselves from the taint of death.

Important personages were buried with great ceremony (below), and precious vessels (such as those pictured above) were placed in their graves.

Enterrement des Rois en Perou.

The bishop of Trujillo and an abbess (left). The imposition of ecclesiastical discipline and the foundation of religious orders were among the main objectives of the conquerors.

A 16th-century engraving of Cuzco (below).

Polo de Ondegardo Discovered That the Places of Veneration, *Huacas,* Were Laid Out in Accordance with Astronomical and Sociological Factors

The term *huaca* refers to a number of very different things: holy sites, monuments, spirits of the air, and statuettes. The Incas aligned the *huaca* sites along imaginary axes that radiated out from their capital city of Cuzco in all directions. A similar system existed at other towns in the territory. Once they had discovered this sacred topography, the Spaniards were able to find many of the *huacas*. They destroyed most of them and kept a close watch on the rites held at those that could not be destroyed, such as mountains or wells.

The number of spiritual *huacas* was, if not infinite, at least very considerable, since each locality and kinship group had its own. The stars were also venerated, and, in some regions, it was thought that every living being had its astral double. The moon was believed to be a woman. During each lunar eclipse, the people—believing the moon had been devoured by a jaguar or a snake—made a great racket in an effort to undo this catastrophe.

Not only heavenly bodies, meteorological phenomena, and certain aspects of nature and topography were considered as *huacas*; there were also small ones—worked stones or statuettes that families passed down

from generation to generation, which looked after the fertility of family members and their land. The term *huaca* is still applied to anything strange, such as twin births, a harelip, or an individual born feet first.

Taqui Onqoy: "Illness Dance"

Hunted down by the *encomenderos* and the priests, neglected by their *caciques*—who preferred to compromise with the invader and take advantage of the situation—and disappointed by the weakness of the Inca resistance led by Manco at Vitcos, the inhabitants of central Peru began to display strange behavior troubling to the Spaniards: They were seized by frenzies and convulsions. Abandoning the cultivation of their fields, the possessed individuals claimed to be inhabited by the *huacas* that had been overlooked since the arrival of the Christians and were thought to be wandering through

A textile doll of the pre-Inca Chancay culture (above).

the air. Emaciated and thirsty, the *huacas* were in search of animate beings to enter, so as to speak through their mouths.

The possessed thought of themselves as living *huacas* and received offerings from the faithful. They delivered prophecies and announced the return of the Inca and its inevitable corollary: the definitive disappearance of the Spaniards, together with their animals, their wheat, their weapons, and their religion.

This movement gradually faded away with the confirmed fall of the Inca state of Vitcos. But other varieties of unorthodox behavior continued to appear sporadically. The unhappy natives also discovered how to mask their own spiritual practices in the guise of Christian rites, a practice known as syncretism. Despite the vigilance of the Spanish ecclesiastical authorities, these composite rites resisted repression. The feast of Corpus Christi, for example, corresponded to that of the sun, and the worshipers used this coincidence to make offerings to their *huacas,* which they hid behind the figure of a saint or of Christ.

Contemporary Andean folklore is filled with malevolent spirits. The Spanish chroniclers of the 16th century claimed that the ancient Peruvians had a conception of the devil, whom they called *supay.* Below: A 19th-century print of a festival at Lima.

Because Spanish Depictions of Saint James Often Showed Him with Thunder, the Natives Saw Him as a Hispanic Version of Thunder and Lightning, a Cosmic Being Who for Them Had Always Been a Subject of Adoration

The Andean peoples abandoned the old names and even began to give the Christian name James to their baptized children, a fact that did not escape the notice of the priests, who forced them to change James to the innocuous Diego.

Other ancient festivals, like that of La Citua, continued to be celebrated in remote places. During the reign of the Incas, this imposing rite had taken place in the month of August, when the first rains began to fall. Then its function had been to banish illness and misfortune which, it was thought, were punishments for

Although the Spanish religious authorities understood that the festivals had spiritual significance for the natives, they did not ban them, but limited themselves to condemning their "diabolical" purpose.

EL OTA BO ÍNGA
VIRACOCHA INGA

Reyno — Iquinae
coxca ona — Dimiua

yatyos; xauya
Xula Goro

wyracocha

neglecting the Inca or the *huacas.* On these occasions, strangers were chased out of town along with all those who had any kind of deformity, a clear sign of misconduct or sin. Then people dressed in warrior costumes would exhort evil to leave the town. Grouped in four squadrons, they set off in the direction of each of the four quarters of the empire to strike their invisible enemy. Once they had reached the frontier of the territory of Cuzco, they washed in a river to purify themselves. In the evening they lit straw torches and waved them like palm fronds. The festival lasted several days and comprised numerous purification rites, the aim of which was not so much to eliminate all pathogenic or malevolent elements as simply to drive them away. Similarly, the festival's aim was not to destroy evil but to push it out beyond the town's boundaries.

The Spanish ecclesiastical authorities established strict rules for effectively combating this "idolatry." This term (which the clergy coined by analogy with ancient paganism) designated indigenous beliefs, rites, customs, cults, and ceremonies as the many signs of the aberration into which the devil had led the credulous natives. To the Spanish colonists, idolatry—practiced by the civilizations of the ancient world—was not a regression but a perversion of the spirit.

Many Chroniclers Felt That the Natives Had an Intuition of God Through the Figure of Viracocha, a Mythical Being Who Was Believed to Have Emerged from Lake Titicaca

According to legend, Viracocha created the first humans from clay prototypes, which he modeled after himself,

The church of Santo Domingo (opposite), built on the ancient temple of the sun in Cuzco, is particularly striking testimony to the syncretism between the ancient Inca religion and Christianity. Left: A depiction of the Inca god Viracocha by Felipe Guamán Poma de Ayala.

A terra-cotta figurine (below).

before being exiled from the world of the living by the ingratitude of his creatures. Under the influence of Christianity, this civilizing hero took on the traits of an apostle, or even of God himself, who had come to preach "the good news" in these lost valleys of the Cordilleras.

The sun, ancestor of the Incas, held the most important place in the pantheon of idolatry. The Cuzco dynasties imposed the cult on all the conquered peoples, and at Cuzco they built a temple devoted entirely to the worship of the sun. Known as the Coricancha, its doors were covered in gold, and like so many other cult shrines, the Coricancha was desecrated and plundered when the Spaniards arrived. Part of the wealth from these temples formed Atahualpa's ransom, and pillage took care of the rest. Such vandalism must be ascribed to the soldiers rather than the clergy, for the latter mostly contented themselves with transforming the pagan buildings into churches. For example, the foundations of the Coricancha, still visible today, are surmounted by the church of Santo Domingo.

The Clergy Systematically Destroyed Any Object That Could Form Part of an Idolatrous Cult or Serve as a Reminder of One

Feathers, ritual fabrics, conch shells (the musical instruments used in festivities), and even cradles fed the purifying pyres, while hymns were banned and protective stones were thrown into the water or smashed.

At sites in the mountains where the natives left offerings to appease the *huacas,* the priests would set up crosses. But the clergy themselves knew that sometimes

"In removing all these things not merely from their eyes but even more so from their hearts, with continual sermons and the catechism, it is to be very greatly feared that roots which are so deep and so ancient have not entirely been drawn up or torn out with the first ploughing, and in order to prevent them growing again, to uproot them definitively, a second and third ploughing will be necessary. It is true that all the Indians visited remain informed, corrected and cured, and that the children will be better than their fathers, and the grandchildren better than their fathers and grandfathers...."
Pablo José de Arriaga
The Extirpation of Idolatry in Peru, 1621

This French ballet costume (left) from the time of Louis XIV (known as the Sun King) equates the regent with an Inca priest.

Sculpture of a musician playing a *quena,* a sort of clarinet (above).

The dedication of Spanish priests eventually succeeded in completely suppressing the ancient religion, and today the Catholic church in South America is among the most powerful in the world. A priest gives absolution to a dying native (left).

very violent storms would break out in the highlands and tear out these signs that the mountain did not tolerate.

Just as they had always fought against the native funerary customs, the clergy also set about controlling the other rites of passage: birth, puberty, and marriage. In order to achieve a radical conversion of the natives to Christianity, they had to bring about a total break with the past. So the clerical authorities forced the natives— not always successfully—to adopt European first names instead of traditional ones, suppressed the puberty ritual for boys of the nobility, and banned polygamy.

To enforce this cultural reform, the priests related edifying stories and used pictures that depicted the horrors of hell and the punishments of purgatory.

To Replace the Idols They Had Destroyed, the Priests Gave out Rosaries and Images of Saints with Curative Powers

Finally, they induced the converts to join religious confraternities protected by a saint. But the natives managed to reconcile the practice of Christianity with their ancient mountain cults and reconstituted, within the framework of the confraternity, the old kinship groups that had been disrupted by the Spanish reorganization of society. Although the clergy had eradicated a good number of idolatries, they had to resign themselves to tolerate a syncretic Catholicism that would survive into the 20th century.

In the eyes of the Roman Catholic priests, "ministers of the devil" were even more dangerous than objects. In this category they lumped the keepers of the *huacas,* healers, soothsayers, priests attached to the great temples, wizards, and sorcerers, even though their respective roles were quite distinct. For example, a sorcerer was generally a ne'er-do-well who used poisoned food or manipulated objects with evil powers to induce death or terrible

diseases—practices which had in fact been condemned by the Incas themselves and which incurred the death penalty. In reality, those bent on eradicating the old religion were aware of the difference between an herbalist, a keeper of mummies, a priest who performed sacrifices, and a sorcerer, but they viewed them all with the same intolerant reprobation.

Among the Characters the Clergy Most Abhorred Were Those Who Had the Ability to Understand the Language of the *Huacas,* and Who Could Thus Interpret the Signs of Nature and Predict the Future

These intermediaries between invisible powers and humans were often chosen because of a particular personality trait. Similarly, survivors of lightning strikes were thought to have powers of clairvoyance. To

The Spanish temperament had always been preoccupied with the paraphernalia of death, and in Central and South America they found peoples with curiously similar obsessions. This engraving (opposite) shows the Festival of the Dead at Cuzco.

Every community had to assign a cook, a baker, and a gardener to the local Spanish priest. In addition, the priest received various payments: tithes and first fruits levied at harvest time; parish rights for the celebration of baptisms, marriages, and funerals, as well as money for masses in honor of the saints (gifts that were theoretically voluntary); and a salary paid by the community. In this 19th-century painting a priest is visited by three women of Lima.

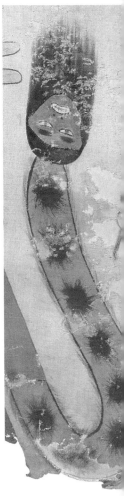

communicate with the *huacas,* the soothsayers used intoxicating substances such as *vilca,* a hallucinogenic plant. The intermediaries then uttered their prophecies in a special tone of voice, supposedly of the *huacas* speaking through their mouths. The muteness of the saints, whom the natives identified as Christian *huacas,* struck them as odd, especially as they were represented in painting and sculpture with an absolutely terrifying realism.

There were other important characters in the native belief system. The keepers of the *huacas,* for example, organized public confessions during which people admitted their faults—such as not having respected the rites; not having made offerings to the *huacas* or the solar divinity; having profaned the chastity of the women reserved for the Inca; having killed or stolen; or, finally, having spoken ill of the Inca. Only the Incas and the Cuzco nobility were allowed to confess in secret.

This enumeration of faults inevitably evokes the Catholic practice of confessing sins. Just as the ancient work discipline facilitated the Andean population's subjugation to the colonial system, so this traditional moral rigor made its conversion to Christianity easier.

To Treat the Most Common Illnesses, Inca Medicine Used Remedies of Animal or Mineral Origin, as well as Plants from Different Ecological Zones

In almost every society, those responsible for treating and curing illnesses enjoy great respect, and the native Andean healers were not exceptions. However, judging from Quechua vocabulary for the parts of the human body, it seems that the anatomical knowledge among the Andean peoples was very limited. This did not prevent them from practicing trepanation, however, which

A funerary doll of the Chancay culture (above left).

In the imagery of the early Andean civilizations, the jaguar embodies a very ancient cult. At the time of the Incas, this animal was associated with the lowlands and their savage inhabitants. At left is a painted textile from Nazca.

Funerary masks such as the one above (from the Chancay culture) could be made of cloth, metal, or even human skin taken from a noble of high rank.

The Dance of the Lions (left), an Inca festival, shown in a 17th-century illustration. Above: The plains beneath the great volcano, Chimborazo, painted by German naturalist Alexander von Humboldt (1769–1859).

involved making small holes in the skull using very fine copper knives. Despite the dangerous nature of this operation, at least some patients must have survived, because skulls have been found in which the orifice had partially closed up again.

Itinerant healers traveled around the Andean provinces with their precious herbs and drugs. The Spaniards took an immediate interest in these medicinal plants because they, too, used herbal tonics for the

treatment of various maladies. European plants began to rival the native species in the late 16th century, but even though the peasants gradually adapted these new species to their own needs, they continued to favor their existing pharmacopoeia; even the Europeans tended to prefer the indigenous remedies. The parish priests played an important role in disseminating the Incas' knowledge of herbal medicine, because it was they who finally wrote down the recipes that for centuries had circulated orally throughout the country.

In contrast to therapeutic practices were those that touched on sorcery, particularly rituals designed to put an end to one's rivals. In the colonial period, Inca methods of sorcery were supplemented by other techniques brought in by the Spanish as well as by the Spaniards' African slaves. These included dolls modeled in the image of one's enemy, which could be pierced with arrows to bring about that person's death. The Europeans circulated books of spells and enriched them with information obtained from the Andean peasants. For instance, it was widely believed that the *huacas* produced malevolent emanations that shriveled the violators of tombs. Indeed, it is probable that it was partly through the sharing of medicine and sorcery that the different peoples coexisting in the Andes from the 16th century onward developed a common language.

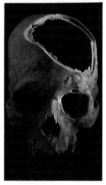

Trepanation was practiced not only on living subjects but also on the dead, in order to pour substances into the skull that would preserve it from putrefaction.

Two hundred years after Pizarro's arrival, the Andean world was plunged into profound misery, crushed by taxes and forced labor and exasperated by the arrogance of the Spanish. There were rumblings of rebellion. The time had come to shake off the colonial yoke and restore the kingdom of the Incas.

CHAPTER V
THE INCA'S RETURN

By a sort of retrospective iconography, this 17th-century representation of an Inca (opposite) shows him with the headdress of Atahualpa and the sun symbol on his breast but bearing the Christian cross. At right, a conquistador raises aloft his cross.

On their arrival in the Andes, the Spaniards had found a society that was hardworking, disciplined, even rigorous, but also strongly hierarchical. The ruling class was made up of powerful nobles, formerly chiefs in charge of independent provinces but later, following Inca expansion, vassals of the Inca himself. The lords of Chimor, Chincha, and Quito had all been made heads of important noble households. In the northern Andes, these elites controlled the trade routes between the mountains and the lowlands; in the Lake Titicaca region they possessed immense herds of vicuñas and llamas; and on the coast they were masters of the maritime trade.

Keros were vessels of gold or painted wood (as above) that the Incas used for their ritual libations. Of similar ritual significance were such symbols of power as feather crowns or fine fabrics (detail of a Paracas textile, left). Below are two pre-Inca vessels.

In return for his power, each lord, or *cacique,* had a certain number of obligations to fulfill, such as generosity toward his subjects and the redistribution of some of the resources that resulted from his position. Although hereditary, this position did not necessarily obey the rule of primogeniture (the Spaniards imposed this later), and the seigneury could just as well be passed to a nephew—the son of the *cacique*'s sister, for example.

The notion of private ownership of land did not exist before the colonial period. The wealth of the *caciques* was measured instead in terms of the numbers of houses, wives, servants, and animals they held—together with ritual objects that in our eyes may have little value, such as ornaments, bead necklaces, *keros* (vases used for ritual libations), feathers, little bells, shells, and, of course, fabrics. The *caciques'* servants, or *yana,* were either hereditary servants or slaves.

According to Legend, These *Yana* Had Been Rebels Against the Inca Who Had Been Reprieved by the Coya, His Principal Wife, and Condemned to Work for the Lords or the State

In the Aymara kingdoms of Lake Titicaca, the *yana* watched over herds that numbered more than twenty thousand animals. Whether servants, serfs, or herders, the *yana* were exempt from tribute, and some enjoyed even greater privileges, especially those who lived in the entourage of the Inca and his close relatives.

Nevertheless, the *yana* remained of inferior rank because, being detached from their native community and belonging to no particular territorial or kinship group, they were deprived of an identity.

After the Spanish conquest, the *yana* kept their ancient privileges and were thus exempted from all forced labor. As they had no access to community land, however, they were forced to attach themselves to the great estates of the Spaniards, forming the nucleus of a servile workforce

In addition to traditional status objects, the *caciques* acquired Spanish furniture, including chests like this one (above), which bears witness to the emergence of a notion of private property, previously unknown among the Incas. They contained fabrics, Catholic liturgical objects, silks, title deeds, and genealogies.

that was swelled through the centuries by a stream of peasants driven by poverty to seek jobs on the haciendas.

Since the Spaniards belonged to a society founded on

class distinctions, they respected the status of the Inca nobles and the *caciques,* although they did not grant them political autonomy. Pizarro lived maritally with two of Atahualpa's wives, first Doña Ines and then Doña Angelina, by whom he had three children, one of them given the composite name of Francisco Pizarro Yupanqui. Other conquistadors took as wives women belonging to the Cuzco dynasties or the regional seigneuries. But while such unions with the indigenous elite undoubtedly took place, they never became common practice. On the other hand, the acculturation of the *caciques'* children was systematic from the 16th century onward, and religious schools were established where they were taught the writing, language, and manners of the Spanish nobility.

The *Caciques* and Their Families Dressed in Spanish Style, Spoke Fluent Spanish, and Professed Catholicism

It was the duty of the *caciques* to collect tribute and represent the indigenous community over which they exercised authority. For the Spanish authorities they were the indispensable intermediaries who could

The *yana,* the Inca's appointed servants (shown in these 19th-century illustrations), became servants of the Spaniards in the colonial period.

The school in Cuzco for the children of the native nobility was run by priests. The twenty or so pupils dressed in Spanish style with a green uniform and a black hat. They wore their hair down to their shoulders, as a mark of their status (short hair was a mark of disgrace to the Incas, and the missionaries often used this punishment to intimidate idolaters). The lessons consisted essentially of theology and Catholic doctrine.

recruit a workforce. Their roles as liaisons expedited their integration into the colonial world, and they often used their privileged positions to acquire land and livestock, benefiting from the Spanish law that regulated access to private property. In southern Peru and the region of Potosí in Bolivia, many of these officials became powerful merchants.

But the *caciques* remained torn between the two

A... Yndio Principal de, Quito trage de Gala.

B... Arbol de Guabas Machetonas. y, Bejugillas.

C... Fagsos Fruta y elmodo como se enreda su rama

D... Arbol, y Fruta delas Guayabas.

E... Yndio del Campo.

Although the native Andean populations were cruelly exploited by Spanish landowners and businessmen, they were of scholarly interest to philosophers and early scientists. This painting, and the two on the following pages, were made in about 1700 to illustrate the peoples and products of the New World. This page shows an inhabitant from Cuzco dressed in Spanish fashion.

Rural Native

This member of Yumbo tribe has few of the attributes of Spanish civilization. His headdress, quiver, and belt are adorned with feathers, and he wears strings of shells round his neck and thighs. He is dressed for a feast (hence the coloring on his cheeks) and holds a bow and a spear. The fruits include bananas, plantains, and pineapples—which, according to the painting's caption, are "very aromatic and tasty." The painting typifies a certain view of colonial power but should not be seen as a faithful image of social reality in 18th-century Peru.

A. Yndio Yumbo
    de las immediaciones
    de Quito con su trage
    de Plumas y Cormillos de
    Animales de Caza de que vsã
    quando estan de Pala

B. Platano, Arvol que Produce
    los de la Casta de Guineos con
    su Fruto, y son los mas delicados,

C. Platano Arvol q̃ los Produce lla
    mados Dominicos, que no son de
    tan delicado savor como los pri
    meros.

D. Arvol que Produce las Papaias,
    y su Fruta entera y avierta, es
    saludable.

E. La Piña consu Mata cuierta y en
    tera, Es Fruta muĩ ȭ lorosa y
    Gustosa

A. Yndia en trage de Gala.
B. Yndia del Canpo con su Paba Pecal.
C. Arbol de Aguacates, y su Fruta.
D. Arbol de chilguacanes con su Fruta en, tera, y partida.
E. Arbol de Chamburos con su Fruta en, tera, y abierta.
F. Mamey con sus ojas, y fruta abierta.

Inhabitants of Town and Country

There was a sharp distinction between urban and rural dwellers. The former, who frequently intermarried with Spaniards, adopted European costume and manners (though this lady, rather surprisingly, wears no shoes). In the background, bent under a heavy burden, is a poor peasant with his dog. On the table and in the basket are fruits unknown in Europe before the conquest—such as avocados—as well as a larger variety of the familiar strawberry.

cultures, and they preserved some features from the past, such as a defiant pride befitting the great lords of old. They liked to drink, though not to excess, and were ready to display enormous generosity. They were inordinately fond of ostentatious luxury, coats of arms, and music, and they maintained ties of spiritual kinship with their subjects by means of patronage.

To limit the power of the *caciques,* the colonial administration created a parallel power within the indigenous villages, along the lines of the Spanish municipal council. At the head of this organization was the mayor (*alcalde*), who controlled the distribution of land and kept a watchful eye on the conduct of the natives. Along with the *cacique,* he was responsible for collecting tribute, and was assisted by two *regidores,* or municipal magistrates. Finally, the *alguacils* acted as police. The members of the municipal council were elected annually. "Commoners"—that is, peasants—could be andidates, but only on condition that they were good Christians and would cooperate with the Spanish authorities, for the councils were under the orders of the *corregidor,* a colonial magistrate at the provincial level.

There Was Much Overlapping of Administrative and Religious Authority

This phenomenon, which is characteristic of the rural colonial world, wove solid ties between the village officials and the parish priest. The prestige of the members of the municipal council, and of all those who wished to become members, depended on their participation in the cult of the saints: It was up to the *priostes* (those "appointed" to a saint) to gather the money needed for the celebration of the festival. The more sumptuous the festivities, the greater the esteem enjoyed by its organizers.

The 17th-century clergy attempted to suppress the ancient festivals in order to erase the tradition of the *huacas* from the memory of their charges. These were replaced by others that intermingled customs

The African slaves of the Spaniards were frequently better off than the native Peruvians, who were technically free. Don Francisco de Arobe, a former slave who survived a shipwreck, had, with his brothers, become *cacique* of the Cayapa population of Esmeraldas (in Ecuador). This picture, painted in Quito by a local artist, shows them dressed in Spanish style with the traditional golden ornaments of the natives. Opposite: The bullfight, a spectacle introduced into Peru by the Spanish.

of the past with those of European origin. Carnival festivities, for example, which are pagan by definition, were adopted very quickly by the country peasants. Other celebrations had much in common with the theatrical performances then highly prized in Spain, but were adapted to local practices. Bullfights and equestrian games were also popular. The ancient rituals became clandestine or gradually gave way to festival-spectacles which, in their turn, became fixed in folkloric tradition.

But the noise of the festivals was not enough to muffle the sound of anger that was growing throughout the country— for the burden of forced labor and the development of large estates at the expense of community lands had reduced the natives to poverty.

Toward the Middle of the 18th Century, Rebellions Against Spanish Oppression Broke Out Throughout the Andean Region, from Ecuador to Argentina

In the forest zones of Tarma and Jauja in Peru, a man named Juan Santos Atahualpa fought the Spaniards for nearly twenty years, from 1742 to 1761. He proclaimed that he had come to reconstitute the kingdom of the Incas with its native, mixed-race, and black sons. He relied heavily on the help of the English, for political and commercial tensions had by this time pitted Spain against England. The latter was eager to establish trading links with the continent whose resources had been thus far monopolized by Spain. In the region of Huarochiri, natives who had rebelled against fiscal abuses threw the *corregidor* and his brother-in-law from the top of a cliff. At Quito, the frenzy even affected parishes which had until then been considered peaceful.

But it was in southern Peru and the Bolivian region of Potosí that the insurrection shook the foundations of the viceroyship. The rural masses there were kept in a state of ignorance and degradation by the *corregidores* and the priests. Meanwhile, many of the Inca *caciques* enjoyed the benefits of refined education, which would eventually backfire on the oppressor. One such beneficiary was José Gabriel Condorcanqui, a principal figure in the anti-Spanish insurrection. Condorcanqui was a *cacique* from Tinta and a direct descendant via his mother of Felipe Topa Amaru, the last Inca, who had been executed by the viceroy Francisco de Toledo in 1572. Raised in a Jesuit college, Condorcanqui read Latin fluently and spoke Spanish just like a Spaniard.

Condorcanqui laid claim before a tribunal to the seigneury of Tinta, which he said came down to him from his ancestors. Then he took the name of Topa Amaru II, to underline his descent from his murdered forefather.

Administrative posts were filled by natives elected by their community rather than members of the elite. But access to these posts was closely tied to the candidates' commitment to Christianity. In this way, the municipal system overlapped with a religious hierarchy.

Opposite: A native official takes part in a religious procession with two children dressed as angels. Below: An officer of the militia.

Topa Amaru II, a Merchant and Owner of a Troop of Mules, Traveled Around the Southern Andes Without Alarming the Spanish Authorities

With his ally Tomas Catari, legitimate *cacique* of Chayanta, Topa Amaru carefully prepared the general insurrection. It broke out in 1780 and spread like lightning. The rebel armies numbered up to 80,000 natives, together with many mixed-race sympathizers. Topa Amaru's program was certain to alarm the Spanish monarchy, since he planned to abolish the inhuman mining labor practices and forced labor in general, as well as to restore the Inca empire.

Topa Amaru challenged the political legitimacy of the Spanish, whom he considered usurpers. He denounced the bad *corregidores*—"enemies of God, atheists,

Fighting alongside the regular troops of revolutionary leaders José Francisco de San Martín (1778–1850) and Simon Bolívar (1783–1830), native guerrillas played an important role in the struggles for the emancipation of Peru, which lasted from 1819 to 1824. Below: Bolívar on campaign in Llanos (Colombia).

Calvinists, and Lutherans, idolaters of gold and silver";
he attributed their villainy to the baseness of their
nature. But the peasants were soon abandoned by the
townspeople, who, although hostile to the Spanish
monarchy, had no wish to join a movement that was so
radical and—worse still—native. In 1781 Topa Amaru
was arrested and tortured.

The last Inca underwent a death even more horrible
than that of his ancestor. After witnessing the executions
of his wife, his son, and his companions, he had his tongue
cut out and was tied to four horses to be torn apart. But
his body would not tear, and his persecutors were forced
to have his head cut off. Finally, his limbs were severed
and sent to the four centers that had fomented the
rebellion—the punishment thus acknowledging the
structure of the empire of the Four Quarters.

Portrait of Simon
Bolívar (above).
The responsibilities of
a racially mixed
population constituted
the starting point of
Bolívar's political and
social theories. "Our
population," he said,
"is a mixture of Africa
and America rather than
an emanation from
Europe. The majority
of indigenous peoples
were exterminated. The
Europeans mixed with
Americans and Africans.
Whereas we all have the
same mother, our fathers
are foreigners and
differ in their origins and
their blood, as well as in
the color of their skin,
which places obligations
of the highest importance
upon us."

The Spaniards' Revenge Was Not Assuaged by the Inca's Death: His Relatives, as Distant as Fourth Cousins, Were Hunted Down and Murdered

The 18th century ended with the most brutal repression that the native populations had ever suffered. But the victory of the Spanish authorities was short-lived. A few decades later, the Creoles (descendants of Spaniards born on American soil, who were looked upon as second-class by their compatriots in Madrid) organized a revolution against the Spanish monarchy. This uprising—directed by revolutionary heroes José Francisco de San Martín and Simon Bolívar—led to the emancipation of the old colonies. Between 1822 and 1824, after several bloody wars, Greater Colombia, Peru, and Bolivia won their independence. The patriots were inspired by the ideals of the French Revolution and wanted to make the natives into citizens. Peru's "Protector" San Martín abolished forced labor there in 1821, even before achieving a final victory. But the new republican regime, founded on the concept of the private ownership of land—which it considered to be the best means of tying citizens to their country—tolled the death knell of the indigenous communities, which gradually lost their legal status and ultimately could not compete with the powerful large estates.

Deprived of community lands, the peasants were now driven to accept the exploitative conditions under the *concertaje* system—a system which, more often than not, put them in debt for life. Receiving an advance from his employer at the start, the native *concierto* was required to work in his employer's fields until he had repaid the debt, plus interest. The so-called economic liberalism of the newly freed Latin American states was, thus, ultimately to turn the native Americans into a proletariat.

After the liberation of the province of the Río de la Plata, the future Argentina, José Francisco de San Martín (opposite) led his army from Chile to Peru. In 1821 he entered Lima and set up a republican government, himself becoming "protector of Peru." At this point Bolívar was at Quito, from whence he controlled all of northern Peru. These two men were completely opposite in character. Bolívar, more ambitious than San Martín, and doubtless a better politician, eventually emerged as the victor. Back in Lima, San Martín resigned in 1822 and set sail for Chile that very evening. The Peruvian congress quickly granted Bolívar full authority to repel a Spanish offensive. At Lima Bolívar promised the independence of Peru (left). San Martín ended his days in exile in France, where he died in 1850 at Boulogne-sur-Mer.

In the 19th century, adventurers, explorers, and gold prospectors from all over the world traveled to Peru to find Vitcos and Vilcabamba. But the two legendary citadels of Inca resistance in the 16th century seemed to have mysteriously vanished. In 1911 Hiram Bingham (1875–1956), an American historian from Yale University, set off to search for the phantom cities.

CHAPTER VI
THE HERITAGE OF THE INCAS

The Andes are a formidable barrier (below, a view of the Cordillera), perhaps still concealing other cities like Machu Picchu (opposite).

Passionately interested in Latin America and an authority on the revolutionary leader Simon Bolívar, Hiram Bingham set out to travel from Lima to Buenos Aires on a mule, thus hoping to cover a large part of Inca territory. The prefect of Apurimac, a province close to Cuzco, told him of ruins lost in the mountains, which the natives called Choqquequirau, the "cradle of gold." Access to these ruins was extraordinarily difficult because there was no bridge over the Apurimac River, and most of the area was covered by forest. Nonetheless tempted by adventure, Bingham prepared an expedition in the hope of discovering Vitcos and Vilcabamba, believed to be the two last forest refuges of the Inca Manco and his sons, who had resisted the Spaniards until 1572.

The information at his disposal was pretty thin and, moreover, contradictory. First there were the writings of the 16th-century chroniclers, including the Inca Titu Cusi himself, son of Manco and brother of the unfortunate Topa Amaru. Titu Cusi testifies to the struggle of the last Incas, who had retreated to the Amazonian piedmont. However, another source, an Augustinian missionary and chronicler named Father Antonio de Calancha, had located Vitcos at a place where a white rock overhung a waterhole, near a temple of the sun. These were pretty meager clues with which to find the traces of an Inca city, buried under the tropical vegetation.

The slopes and eastern piedmont of the central Andes are mostly sheer and deeply cut by narrow valleys. The only natural passages are the rivers, including the Urubamba (a photograph by Bingham, above), but these are punctuated by impassable rapids and falls. The site of Machu Picchu was discovered and excavated by foreigners (opposite, Hiram Bingham and his native guide) only after prolonged effort and hardship.

Although Bingham Was Not the First Explorer to Seek Manco's Capital—There Were Many Before Him—He Was the Luckiest

In the early 20th century, the inhabitants of the village of Ollantaytambo, built beside the Urubamba River, were still living in Inca dwellings. Traveling through the region, Bingham found these and numerous other Inca remains. One day, after questioning workers in the valley's sugar-cane plantations, he finally found—at a spot called Rosaspata—a white rock overhanging a spring with black waters. Nearby was a temple of the sun. This sinister place precisely matched Calancha's description. Bingham had found Vitcos.

This discovery encouraged him to undertake a difficult expedition into the eastern valleys. He was certain that the remains of Rosaspata were not those of "Vilcabamba the ancient," Manco's capital. Based on further information from native plantation workers, Bingham finally reached Choqquequirau, where he found a real fortress with paved roads and buildings of stones that had been fitted together perfectly with no mortar, by means of a remarkable technique. Other visitors had been there before the American, and Bingham discovered signatures carved into the walls, including that of a Frenchman, Eugène de Sartigues, who had evidently passed through in 1834.

This was a great discovery for Bingham; nonetheless, when, returning from this expedition, he admitted to the prefect of Apurimac that he had found no gold, there was general disappointment.

Interest in the Incas at This Time Revolved Almost Exclusively Around the Gold in Their Tombs —The Greed of the Republicans Matching That of the Conquistadors

Bingham persisted. He wanted to find the city of Vilcabamba, which, according to 16th-century chroniclers, must be even farther away—"a little further along," as his local guides kept repeating. Listening to even the craziest rumors, Bingham forged a path through suffocating gorges and climbed up to glaciers only to

Father Calancha reported that, near Vitcos, there was a "white stone" from which a spring arose. There, the *huaca* called "parantin" was reputed to have delivered his prophecies. The Augustinian friars declared war on the "demon," and exorcised the rock. Hiram Bingham found just such a rock (opposite).

In the time of the Incas, the monumental fortress of Ollantaytambo (left) had several functions. In addition to watching over the Urubamba Valley and keeping a lookout for dreaded incursions by forest tribes, it was an agricultural center, like its neighbor Pisac. To judge by the quality of the buildings, water channels, and sanctuaries, it probably also served as a residence for the Inca or his family. The style of its stonework suggests that Ollantaytambo was built in the second half of the 15th century.

In the Shadow of Huayna Picchu

The jagged contours of the mountain summit, together with the very dense vegetation that surrounded it, combined to isolate Machu Picchu from the outside world. The site was secluded not only from the Cuzco region but also from the lowlands—cut off by the gorge of the Pongo Moenike, which is impassable in the rainy season. Hence the remarkable nature of this urban settlement. According to legend, Machu Picchu was built for the virgins of the sun, the *aclla*. Father Calancha reported in 1560 that two Augustinian friars, who had been invited to Vilcabamba by the Inca himself, underwent tough tests aimed at shaking their chastity: Every evening, women were sent to tempt them, but apparently in vain. Today, however, archaeologists give little credence to the idea that Machu Picchu was a shelter for the Inca's *aclla*. Some scholars identify Vilcabamba not at Machu Picchu but with Espiritu Pampa, a site in the more hospitable environment of the headwaters of the Amazon.

A World in the Sky

Whatever the mysteries surrounding its origins and purpose, Machu Picchu was probably built on the model of the traditional Andean village. Left: An artist's reconstruction of Machu Picchu as it appeared during the reign of the Incas. Sometimes aligned on narrow terraces, or gathered in groups of four, six, or even ten around a communal courtyard, the dwellings were linked by narrow alleys. Large open squares occupied the village center, while around the edge there stretched vast enclosures for livestock and terraces for growing maize. Outside each house, in the little courtyard, were the great millstone (where grain was crushed), the bulkiest agricultural implements, the store of llama dung used for fuel, the textile workshop, and, exposed to the sun and frost, the potatoes used to make *chuño*. Strips of *ch'arki*, or dried meat, were also hung outside, dangling from a rope.

descend once more to the Amazonian furnace. After losing his way at least once, he finally passed from the valley of the Apurimac into that of the Urubamba. As he approached his goal the locals' descriptions became more and more precise.

The American was astonished by what appeared to be their indifference toward the ruins—ruins that, in his opinion, should have stirred their deepest emotions. But to the inhabitants of the Andes, the archaeological remains inspired terrible fear. As a result of the teachings of the 16th-century evangelists, the locals were especially fearful of human bones, which they had been led to believe could inflict horrible illnesses. One archaeologist reported that the workers he employed in his excavations refused to unearth ancient tombs, out of fear of "being crippled by the vapor of the corpses."

After an arduous walk and an exhausting climb, Bingham reached his destination. The spectacle that met his eyes, one July day in 1911, more than compensated for all his pains: He had discovered Machu Picchu. He entered a magnificent city built on an eagle's nest, where streets, staircases, monuments, temples, and houses were set in a sumptuous landscape. Opposite rose the peak of Huayna Picchu, which was also covered in ruins.

Is Machu Picchu Manco's City of Vilcabamba? So Thought Bingham, as He Marveled at the Perfection and Beauty of Its Architecture

Machu Picchu had not been lost to everyone, to judge by the disorder in its tombs. Manco's treasure had disappeared. No one knows whether gold prospectors had pillaged it, or whether the last Inca, the young Topa Amaru, had taken part of his ancestor's riches away with him.

Instead of treasure, Bingham made other fascinating discoveries. Besides the grandeur of the site, he was struck by the beauty of the construction of the stone monuments, which formed an unusual grouping. No other civilization in the world had managed to assemble such enormous blocks so perfectly. The blocks were cut with bronze or stone tools,

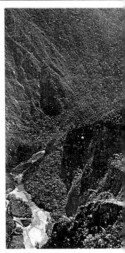

Was Machu Picchu a fortified post to control access to Cuzco? A kind of convent dedicated to the virgins of the sun? The last refuge of the Inca Manco (the puppet ruler placed on the throne by the Spaniards who then revolted against his masters)? Few places have inspired more hypotheses or interpretations than Machu Picchu. Today it is the most visited site in South America. Above: A photograph of Machu Picchu and the Urubamba Valley taken by Hiram Bingham. Opposite: The same valley today.

"Immediately in front, on the north side of the valley, was a great granite cliff rising two thousand feet sheer. To the left was the solitary peak of Huayna Picchu, surrounded by seemingly inaccessible precipices. On all sides were rocky cliffs. Beyond them cloud-capped, snow-covered mountains rose thousands of feet above us."

Hiram Bingham
Lost City of the Incas
1948

and the ridges rubbed together until they fit together like a jigsaw puzzle. But how the Incas could transport and raise such masses without wheels or pulleys remains an enigma.

Bingham found many two-story houses with trapezoidal doors in a remarkable state of preservation. Perhaps the strangest monuments he stumbled upon were a rounded temple, probably consecrated to the sun; a big square, alongside which stood the

Above: Inca houses were small and contained only one room and one door. Inside, trapezoidal niches were cut into the walls. Windows were rare. The beauty of the stonework contrasts with the smallness of the dwelling. Even today, the house is simply the place where one sleeps and seeks protection from the cold.

Left: Machu Picchu's city gate as Bingham found it.

"temple with three windows"; and finally the *intihuatana* (which, in Quechua, literally means "the hitching post of the sun"). The *intihuatana* is a kind of solar clock. It was here, at the winter solstice, when the sun declined and seemed to want to abandon humankind, that a priest performed a ritual aimed at tying the heavenly body to the stone to prevent its disappearance. Machu Picchu's *intihuatana* only escaped the Spaniards' frenzy of destruction because it was so difficult to reach.

The Discovery of This Site Marks the Pinnacle of the Neo-Inca Craze That Was Spreading Through Peruvian Intellectual Circles at the Beginning of the 20th Century

Peru had by this time been an independent country for a century. Yet, like all new Latin-American states, it was still in search of its identity. It is easy to see why the Incas—whose remnants aroused great admiration throughout the world—acquired an emblematic value for all of the country's diverse populations. With Bingham's discovery, the Incas became a positive national symbol.

Some structures were especially designed for astronomical observations, such as the *intihuatana* (above, at Machu Picchu) which was similar to a sundial, and the *sucanca,* pillars set up to the east and west of Cuzco to measure solstices. The Incas believed that the sun had two "seats," the main one in the north and a secondary one in the south. The year began with the summer solstice, when the sun settled into its southern seat.

Can One Speak of Continuity Between the Andean Societies Conquered by the Spaniards in 1532 and the Indigenous Peasants and Proletariat of Today?

If one means biological or racial continuity, the answer can only be negative, with a few exceptions: Racial blending, whether desired or simply accepted by the Spaniards, is an indisputable fact. If one means cultural continuity, the answer will again disappoint all those romantics who are fascinated by ancient grandeur.

Evangelization, the transformation of the land system, the modification of the family structure, and the suppression of the indigenous political organization are all factors that, over the centuries, have forced the peoples of the Cordilleras to forge new identities for themselves.

Nevertheless, despite these social upheavals, there is still such a thing as Andean culture, and it is quite unique. So, although it is fruitless to try to find unchanged vestiges of the past, one is compelled to note that neither the conquistadors nor the evangelists were completely successful. The culture of the Andes is no more frozen in time than any other. It never ceases to integrate new elements, re-creating and recasting them, ultimately embellishing a society that is like no other.

The Incas are not a fossilized people. Their image is still vivid in the minds of contemporary peasants who are yet excluded from all political power. Is this Inca image true to history, or does it serve a merely allegorical purpose? No matter. It lives in the hearts of those whom the modern world seems to have forgotten or, at any rate, marginalized. And the memory of Inca resistance, from Manco to José Gabriel Topa Amaru, can still nourish dreams of rebellion.

Both political thinkers and poets have seen contemporary relevance in the Inca story, but perhaps it is among the contemporary peasants that the collective memory of the Incas is kept alive most vividly.

DOCUMENTS

How can we learn about life in a
civilization that has been so brutally crushed?
The writings of conquistadors and travelers—
and accounts of the natives themselves
—shed light on the people of the sun.

The Conquistadors' Testimony

The earliest chroniclers were mainly concerned with the Spaniards' conquest of Peru and the civil wars between factions of conquistadors. But by reading these observations in combination with the testimony of the natives, we can begin to glimpse the grandeur of the Inca empire and the ways and customs of its inhabitants.

Francisco de Xeres was Francisco Pizarro's secretary. It was in 1534 in Cajamarca ("Caxamalca") that he wrote The Conquest of Peru *and gave the following description of the famous meeting between the conquistador and the Inca Atahualpa ("Atabaliba").*

When the Governor saw that it was near sunset, and that Atabaliba did not move from the place to which he had repaired, although troops still kept issuing out of his camp, he sent a Spaniard to ask him to come into the square to see him before it was dark. As soon as the messenger came before Atabaliba, he made an obeisance to him, and made signs that he should come to where the Governor waited.

Presently he and his troops began to move, and the Spaniard returned and reported that they were coming, and that the men in front carried arms concealed under their clothes, which were strong tunics of cotton, beneath which were stones and bags and slings; all of which made it appear that they had a treacherous design.

Soon the van of the enemy began to enter the open space. First came a

Pizarro's house in Cuzco.

squadron of Indians dressed in a livery of different colours, like a chess board. They advanced, removing the straws from the ground, and sweeping the road. Next came three squadrons in different dresses, dancing and singing. Then came a number of men with armour, large metal plates, and crowns of gold and silver. Among them was Atabaliba in a litter lined with plumes of macaws' feathers, of many colours, and adorned with plates of gold and silver. Many Indians carried it on their shoulders on high. Next came two other litters and two hammocks, in which were some principal chiefs; and lastly, several squadrons of Indians with crowns of gold and silver.

As soon as the first entered the open space they moved aside and gave space to the others. On reaching the centre of the open space, Atabaliba remained in his litter on high, and the others with him, while his troops did not cease to enter. A captain then came to the front and, ascending the fortress near the open space, where the artillery was posted, raised his lance twice, as for a signal. Seeing this, the Governor asked the Father Friar Vicente if he wished to go and speak to Atabaliba, with an interpreter?

He replied that he did wish it, and he advanced, with a cross in one hand and the Bible in the other, and going amongst the troops up to the place where Atabaliba was, thus addressed him: "I am a priest of God, and I teach Christians the things of God, and in like manner I come to teach you. What I teach is that which God says to us in this Book. Therefore, on the part of God and of the Christians, I beseech you to be their friend, for such is God's will, and it will be for your good. Go and speak to the Governor, who waits for you."

The Inca Atahualpa, in a late-16th-century illustration by Felipe Guamán Poma de Ayala.

Atabaliba asked for the Book, that he might look at it, and the Priest gave it to him closed. Atabaliba did not know how to open it, and the Priest was extending his arm to do so, when Atabaliba, in great anger, gave him a blow on the arm, not wishing that it should be opened. Then he opened it himself, and, without any astonishment at the letters and paper, as had been shown by other Indians, he threw it away from him five or six paces, and, to the words which the monk had spoken to him through the interpreter, he answered with much scorn, saying: "I know well how you have behaved on the road, how you have treated my Chiefs, and taken the cloth

P izarro entering Cuzco on 15 November 1533. He is met by a huge army.

from my storehouses." The Monk replied: "The Christians have not done this, but some Indians took the cloth without the knowledge of the Governor, and he ordered it to be restored." Atabaliba said: "I will not leave this place until they bring it all to me." The Monk returned with this reply to the Governor. Atabaliba stood up on the top of the litter, addressing his troops and ordering them to be prepared. The Monk told the Governor what had passed between him and Atabaliba, and that he had thrown the Scriptures to the ground.

Then the Governor put on a jacket of cotton, took his sword and dagger, and, with the Spaniards who were with him, entered amongst the Indians most valiantly; and, with only four men who were able to follow him, he came to the litter where Atabaliba was, and fearlessly seized him by the arm, crying out *Santiago*. Then the guns were fired off, the trumpets were sounded,

and the troops, both horse and foot, sallied forth. On seeing the horses charge, many of the Indians who were in the open space fled, and such was the force with which they ran that they broke down part of the wall surrounding it, and many fell over each other. The horsemen rode them down, killing and wounding, and following in pursuit.

The infantry made so good an assault upon those that remained that in a short time most of them were put to the sword. The Governor still held Atabaliba by the arm, not being able to pull him out of the litter because he was raised so high. Then the Spaniards made such a slaughter amongst those who carried the litter that they fell to the ground, and, if the Governor had not protected Atabaliba, that proud man would there have paid for all the cruelties he had committed. The Governor, in protecting Atabaliba, received a slight wound in the hand.

During the whole time no Indian raised his arms against a Spaniard. So great was the terror of the Indians at seeing the Governor force his way through them, at hearing the fire of the artillery, and beholding the charging of the horses, a thing never before heard of, that they thought more of flying to save their lives than of fighting. All those who bore the litter of Atabaliba appeared to be principal chiefs. They were all killed, as well as those who were carried in the other litters and hammocks. One of them was the page of Atabaliba, and a great lord, and the others were lords of many vassals, and his Councillors. The chief of Caxamalca was also killed, and others; but, the number being very great, no account was taken of them, for all who came in attendance on Atabaliba were great lords.

The Governor went to his lodging, with his prisoner Atabaliba, despoiled of his robes, which the Spaniards had torn off in pulling him out of the litter. It was a very wonderful thing to see so great a lord taken prisoner in so short a time, who came in such power. The Governor presently ordered native clothes to be brought, and when Atabaliba was dressed, he made him sit near him, and soothed his rage and agitation at finding himself so quickly fallen from his high estate. Among many other things, the Governor said to him: "Do not take it as an insult that you have been defeated and taken prisoner, for with the Christians who come with me, though so few in number, I have conquered greater kingdoms than yours, and have defeated other more powerful lords than you, imposing upon them the dominion of the Emperor, whose vassal I am, and who is King of Spain and the universal world.

"We come to conquer this land by his command, that all may come to a knowledge of God, and of His Holy Catholic Faith; and by reason of our good object, God, the Creator of heaven and earth and of all things in them, permits this, in order that you may know Him, and come out from the bestial and diabolical life you lead. It is for this reason that we, being so few in number, subjugate that vast host. When you have seen the errors in which you live, you will understand the good we have done you by coming to your land by order of his Majesty. You should consider it to be your good fortune that you have not been defeated by a cruel people, such as you are yourselves, who grant life to none.

"We treat our prisoners and conquered enemies with kindness, and only make war on those who attack us, and being able to destroy them, we refrain from doing so, but rather pardon them. When I had a Chief, the lord of an island, my prisoner, I set him free that henceforth he might be loyal; and I did the same with the Chiefs who were lords of Tumbez and Chilimasa, and others who, being in my power, and deserving death, I pardoned. If you were seized, and your people attacked and killed, it was because you came against us with so great an army, having sent to say that you would come peacefully, and because you threw the Book to the ground in which is written the words of God. Therefore our Lord permitted that your pride should be brought low, and that no Indian should be able to offend a Christian."

After the Governor had delivered this discourse, Atabaliba thus replied: "I was deceived by my Captains, who told me to think lightly of the Spaniards. I desired to come peacefully, but they prevented me, but all those who thus advised me are now dead. I have now seen the goodness and daring of the Spaniards, and that Malçabilica lied in all the news he sent me touching the Christians."

As it was now night, and the Governor saw that those who had gone in pursuit of the Indians were not returned, he ordered the guns to be fired and the trumpets to be sounded to recall them. Soon afterwards they returned to the camp with a great crowd of people whom they had taken alive, numbering more than three thousand. The Governor asked whether they were all well. His Captain-General, who went with them, answered that only one horse had a slight wound.

Francisco de Xeres
The Conquest of Peru (1534)
Translated by Clements R. Markham
1872

Pedro Pizarro, a cousin of Francisco the conquistador, was less than twenty years old when he was in Cajamarca. He wrote this account in 1571, and his information is less precise than that of de Xeres.

I shall relate the war between Atabaliba and Guascar [Huascar] as I heard it from many Indians and important Lords of this land. In this kingdom there were five Lord Incas before the era in which the Spaniards entered it. These began to conquer and rule this land, making themselves Kings of all of it, because before these Lords vanquished it all the land was divided into *behetrias* [independent tribes], although there were some Lords who had small peoples subject to their government, but these were few, and so the *behetrias* were ever bringing war the one against the other. These Indians say that an Inca arose [and became] the first Lord. Some say that he came forth from the island of Titicaca, which is an isle in a lake in the Collao which is seventy leagues in circuit, and in it, at times, there are storms as in the sea. A small fish, somewhat more than a palm long, is raised in the lake. The water is a little saltish. This lake drains into another which is formed in the province of Carangas and Quillacas, almost as great as this other [lake]. No outlet is to be found, nor [is it known] by what way it is drained. It must be understood to reach the sea by underground channels because, to judge by the great quantity of water which enters it, it can not be otherwise. Other Indians say that this first Lord came forth from Tambo. This Tambo· is in Condesuios, six leagues, more or less, from Cuzco. This first Inca, so they say, was called Inca Vira Cocha. They say that he conquered, won and subjected to his rule the country, for

Engraving of Topa Yupanqui, the tenth Inca.

thirty leagues around Cuzco, where this first Inca established himself. This Inca Vira Cocha left one son who was called Topa Inca Yupanqui Pachacuti who, they say, won one hundred leagues, [as well as other sons] Guaina Inca and Amaru Inca. And these two successors conquered as far as Caxamalca. Guaina Capa, who was the fifth descendant of these, went conquering as far as Quito, and his captains, in another direction, as far as Chile and as far as the bay of San Mateo, and it is almost a thousand leagues from one region to the other. These Lords had the custom of taking their own sisters as wives, because they said that no one was worthy of them save themselves. There was a lineage of these sisters who descended by the same line as these Lords, and the sons of these women were the ones who inherited the kingdom, always the oldest son. Then, besides these sisters, these Lords had all the daughters of the *caciques* of the kingdom for their concubines, and these waited upon the great sisters, and in number they were much more than four thousand. Thus all the Indian women who looked comely to them were divided into lots by these sisters who, themselves, were many....

While this Guaina Capa was conquering around Quito, they say he dallied in winning it [Quito] during more than ten years, and he had this Atabaliba by the daughter of the chief Lord of this province of Quito. Having finished the conquest, Guaina Capa commanded that a fortress be built in memory of the victory which he had won, and thus it was the custom to do in all the provinces which they gained. While they were engaged upon this work, there broke out among them a plague of smallpox, never seen among them before, which killed many Indians. And while Guaina Capa was shut up, engaged in the fast which he was wont to make, which took the form of being alone in a room without access to any woman, and without eating either salt or aji, with which they dress their food, and without drinking *chicha* (he was thus for nine days, at other times for three), while Guaina Capa was thus at his fast they relate that three Indians never seen before came in to him. They were very small, like dwarfs. They said to him: Inca, we are come to summon you. And when he saw this vision [and heard] this which they said to him, he cried out to his servants, and as they entered, these three [dwarfs] already mentioned disappeared, and no one saw them save Guaina Capa, and he said to his servants: Who are these dwarfs who came to summon me? And they answered unto him: We have not seen them.

Then said Guaina Capa: I am about to die. And at once he fell ill of the smallpox. While he was thus very ill, they sent messengers to Pachacamac... and the demon spoke through the idol and bade them take him out into the sun, and soon he would become well. Then, when they did so, matters went the other way, and on being placed in the sun, this Guaina Capa died. The Indians say that he was a great friend of the poor, and he ordered that great care should be taken of them throughout the land. They say that he was very affable to his servants, and very grave. They say that he was wont to drink much more than three Indians together, but that they never saw him drunk, and that, when his captains and chief Indians asked him how, though drinking so much, he never got intoxicated, they say that he replied that he drank for the poor, of whom he supported many. And had this Guaina Capa been alive when we Spaniards entered this land, it would have been impossible for us to win it, for he was much beloved by all his vassals. Ten years had passed since his death when we entered the land. And likewise, had the land not been divided by the wars between Guascar and Atabaliba, we would not have been able to enter or win the land unless we could gather one thousand Spaniards for the task, and at that time it was impossible to get together even five hundred Spaniards on account of their scanty numbers and the evil reputation which the country had, as I have said.

Guaina Capa being dead, they raised up as Lord Guascar his son, to whom the kingdom [rightfully] belonged, and who was in Cuzco, for there his father...had left him. But after some years had passed by, and Atabaliba got his growth, and he was in Quito, where his father begot him, as has been said, he had become very manful and bellicose, and for this reason they advised Guascar to summon him and keep him by him [at court]. When Guascar sent to call him, Atabaliba replied to the messengers

Beginning in the 16th century, published accounts of the Spanish conquest were very popular.

Guascar, albeit a bastard, in order to inherit the kingdom from those to whom it belonged, as I have related above, and [they said] that [the rightful heirs] would aid him and would make him the Lord, for it was known that the men of Quito were the most valiant Indians of this kingdom, as indeed they were. Atabaliba, seeing the will of his vassals, caused himself to be raised up as Lord over them and over the Cañares who aided him.

When Guascar received the news of the uprising of his brother Atabaliba, he sent his captains against him with warriors, and at Tomebamba there was a battle between the two forces, at which Atabaliba was made a prisoner by the men of Guascar, and after they had placed him in a house under guard, one night he broke loose, saying that the sun, who was his father, had set him free, and so do all these Lords declare that they were the sons of the sun. [In truth] it was on account of the insufficient guard which was put over him, for until midnight these Indians keep watch vigilantly, but from midnight onward they all go to sleep, and we Spaniards have seen this during our experiences while conquering the country, especially in the region of Cuzco. Having got free, Atabaliba set himself to re-forming his troops, and he went on ever victorious. These Indians say that the reason why Guascar was but little liked was that he was very grave, and he never let himself be seen by his people, nor did he ever come out to eat with them in the plaza, as it was the custom of former Lords to do sometimes, although others say that the chief reason which led to his downfall was that which I shall here set forth. These Lords had the law and custom of taking that one of

of his brother [saying that], as he had to have an Inca there [in Quito] as a governor, they might say [to Guascar] that he [Atabaliba] was there [for the purpose]. Then, Guascar being counselled by his vassals not to allow it, lest he [Atabaliba] rise up in revolt, he [Guascar] sent a second time to summon him, and he replied in the same manner, and the third time he sent to call him he [Guascar] added that if he did not at once obey the orders given to him, he [Guascar] would send for him. The vassals he [Atabaliba] had in Quito through the family of his mother, as I have said, advised him to arise, as he was the Lord, and because, if he went to Cuzco, he would kill his brother, for he also was a son of Guaina Capa, like

Atahualpa's army is massacred by Pizarro at Cajamarca.

their Lords who died and embalming him, wrapping him up in many fine clothes, and to these Lords they allotted all the service which they had had in life, in order that these bundles [mummies] might be served in death as well as they had in life. Their service of gold and silver was not touched, nor was anything else which they had, nor were those who served them [removed from] the house without being replaced, and provinces were set aside to give them support....

Returning now to Guascar, [it is said that] one day becoming angry with these dead people, he said that he was going to have them all buried, and was going to take away from them all that they possessed, and that there were to be no more dead, but only living, for they [the dead] had all that was best in his kingdom. Since, as I have said, the greater part of the chief people were with these [the dead] on account of the many vices which they had there, and they began to hate Guascar, and they say that the captains whom he sent against Atabaliba let themselves be conquered and that others deserted and passed over to him, and for this reason could Atabaliba conquer, for otherwise neither he nor his people were sufficient to vanquish a village, much less a whole kingdom, and so was Guascar taken prisoner, as I have said, by the captains of Atabaliba, and slain.

Pedro Pizarro
Relation of the Discovery and Conquest of the Kingdoms of Peru (1571)
Translated by Philip A. Means, 1921

The Epic of the Conquest

William H. Prescott's History of the Conquest of Peru *(1847) is a masterpiece of narrative history. Prescott had the imagination of a novelist, and, without departing from the documentary records, he contrived to make Pizarro's adventures come alive in his readers' minds. Here he describes the journey from the coast to Cajamarca.*

Pizarro is welcomed to Cuzco.

At early dawn the Spanish general and his detachment were under arms, and prepared to breast the difficulties of the sierra. These proved even greater than had been foreseen. The path had been conducted in the most judicious manner round the rugged and precipitous sides of the mountains, so as best to avoid the natural impediments presented by the ground. But it was necessarily so steep, in many places, that the cavalry were obliged to dismount, and, scrambling up as they could, to lead their horses by the bridle. In many places, too, where some huge crag or eminence overhung the road, this was driven to the very verge of the precipice; and the traveller was compelled to wind along the narrow ledge of rock, scarcely wide enough for his single steed, where a mis-step would precipitate him hundreds, nay, thousands, of feet into the dreadful abyss! The wild passes of the sierra, practicable for the half-naked Indian, and even for the sure and circumspect mule—an animal that seems to have been created for the roads of the Cordilleras—were formidable to the man-at-arms encumbered with his panoply of mail. The tremendous fissures or *quebradas,* so frightful in this mountain chain, yawned open, as if the Andes had been split asunder by some terrible convulsion, showing a broad expanse of the primitive rock on their sides, partially mantled over with the spontaneous vegetation of ages; while their obscure depths furnished a channel for the torrents, that, rising in the heart of the sierra, worked their way gradually into light, and spread over the savannas and green valleys of the *tierra caliente* on their way to the great ocean.

Many of these passes afforded obvious points of defence; and the Spaniards, as they entered the rocky defiles, looked with apprehension lest they might rouse some foe from his ambush. This apprehension was heightened, as, at the summit of a steep and narrow gorge, in which they were engaged, they beheld a strong work, rising like a fortress, and frowning, as it were, in gloomy defiance of the invaders. As they drew near this building which was of solid stone, commanding an angle of the road, they almost expected to see the dusky forms of the warriors rise over the battlements, and to receive their tempest of missiles on their bucklers; for it was in so strong a position, that a few resolute men might easily have held there an army at bay. But they had the satisfaction to find the place untenanted, and their spirits were greatly raised by the conviction that the Indian monarch did not intend to dispute their passage, when it would have been easy to do so with success.

Pizarro now sent orders to his brother to follow without delay; and, after refreshing his men, continued his toilsome ascent, and before nightfall reached an eminence crowned by another fortress, of even greater strength than the preceding. It was built of solid masonry, the lower part excavated from the living rock, and the whole work executed with skill not inferior to that of the European architect.

Here Pizarro took up his quarters for the night. Without waiting for the arrival of the rear, on the following morning he resumed his march, leading still deeper into the intricate gorges of the sierra. The climate had gradually changed, and the men and horses, especially the latter, suffered severely from the cold, so long accustomed as they had been to the sultry climate of the tropics. The vegetation also had changed its character; and the magnificent timber which covered the lower level of the country had gradually given way to the funereal forest of pine, and, as they rose still higher, to the stunted growth of numberless Alpine plants, whose hardy natures found a congenial temperature in the icy atmosphere of the more elevated regions. These dreary solitudes seemed to be nearly abandoned by the brute creation as well as by man. The light-footed vicuña, roaming in its native state, might be sometimes seen looking down from some airy cliff, where the foot of the hunter dare not venture. But instead of the feathered tribes whose gay plumage sparkled in the deep glooms of the tropical forests, the adventurers now beheld only the great bird of the Andes, the loathsome condor, who, sailing high above the clouds, followed with doleful cries in the track of the army, as if guided by instinct in the path of blood and carnage.

At length they reached the crest of the Cordillera, where it spreads out into a bold and bleak expanse with scarce the vestige of vegetation, except what is afforded by the *pajonal,* a dried yellow grass, which, as it is seen from below, encircling the base of the snow-covered peaks, looks, with its brilliant straw-color lighted up in the rays of an ardent sun, like a setting of gold round pinnacles of burnished silver. The land was sterile, as usual in mining districts, and they were drawing near the once famous gold quarries on the way to Caxamalca;… Here Pizarro halted for the coming up of the rear. The air was sharp and frosty; and the soldiers, spreading their tents, lighted fires, and, huddling round them, endeavoured to find some repose after their laborious march.

William H. Prescott
History of the Conquest of Peru
1847

An Inca's Account of Everyday Life

*Garcilaso de la Vega
(1539–1616), author of the*
Royal Commentaries of the
Incas *(1609), was the son of an
Inca princess and a Spanish
captain. Although his view of
Inca justice is somewhat
idealized, his recollections
constitute an authentic
testimony of the Incas' world.*

An Inca hair-cutting ceremony.

*Garcilaso de la Vega, also known as
"el Inca," was born in Peru but moved to
Spain when he was twenty-one. His father,
Sebastián Garcilaso de la Vega y Vargas,
was at one time the governor of Cuzco.
The two-volume* Commentaries *is an
invaluable source of information about
daily life in Peru both before and after
the conquest.*

How Inca Children Were Raised Without Care

Their children were strangely brought up, both those of the Incas and those of the people, whether rich or poor, without any distinction, and with as little care as could be bestowed upon them. As soon as a child was born, they bathed the little creature with cold water before wrapping it in a blanket; and each morning, before it was wrapped up, they washed it with cold water, generally in the open air. And when the mother would show unusual tenderness, she took the water in her mouth and washed the whole of the child's body with it, except the head, and particularly the crown of the head, which they never touched. They said that they did this to accustom the children to the cold and to hard work, and also to strengthen their limbs. They did not loosen the children's arms from the swaddling bands for more than three months, saying that if they were loosened before that time, the arms would become weak. They were always kept tied up in their cradles, which were benches badly made, four feet long, and one foot was shorter than the others, that the child might be able to rock. The seat or litter on which they put the child was made of a thick net, as strong as a board, and the same net went round each side of the cradle, that the child might not fall out.

Neither in giving them milk, nor at any other time, did they ever take them in their arms, for they said that this would make them cry, and want always to be in their mothers' arms and never in their cradles. The mother leant over her child and gave it the breast, and this was done three times a day, in the morning, at noon, and in the evening. They did not give the child milk at any other time, even if it cried, for they said that if they did it would want to be sucking all day long, and become dirty with vomitings, and that when it was a man it would grow up a great eater and a glutton. The animals, they said, did not give milk to their young all day long, but only at certain hours. The mother herself brought up her child, and she was not allowed to give it out to nurse, how great lady so-ever she might be, unless she was suffering from illness; and while she was suckling the child she abstained from sexual relations with her husband, because they said it was bad for the milk, and made the child pine away. They called those who had thus pined away *ayusca*, which is the past participle, and means literally the incapable, or more properly the changeling....

If the mother had sufficient milk to nourish the child, she never gave it any other food until it was weaned, because they said it injured milk; and they kept the children dirty and untidy. When it was time to take the children out of the cradle, in order not to have to carry them, they made holes in the ground, and put the children into them up to their breasts, wrapping them in dirty napkins, and putting a few trifles before them to play with. There they put the child to jump and kick, but they never carried it in their arms, even if it was a son of the greatest *curaca* [native leader] in the kingdom.

When the child could crawl on all fours, it went to one side or the other of its mother to take the breast, and sucked with its knees on the ground, but it was not allowed to get on her lap. And when it wanted the other breast, it had to go round, that the mother might not be obliged to take it in her arms. The mother cared less about child-bearing than about nursing, for in giving birth she went to a stream, or washed with cold water in the house, and washed the house; beginning immediately afterwards to concern herself about her household affairs, as if nothing had happened. They gave birth without the aid of a midwife, and if such a person was ever used, she was more of a sorceress than a midwife. This was the usual custom of the Indian women in Peru, in bearing and nursing their children, without distinction between rich and poor, high and low....

How Incas Counted Using Strings and Knots

Quipu means to knot, or a knot, and it was also understood as an account, because the knots supplied an account of everything. The Indians made strings of various colours. Some were all of one colour, others of two combined, others of three, others more; and these colours, whether single or combined, all had a meaning. The strings were closely laid up in three or four strands, about the girth of an iron spindle, and three quarters of a *vara* long [around two feet]. They were strung on a thicker cord, from which they hung in the manner of a fringe. The thing to which a string referred was understood by its colour: for instance, a yellow string referred to gold, a white one to silver, and a red one to soldiers.

Things which had no colour were

The *quipu*, a device made of knotted strings, was used for keeping accounts.

arranged according to their importance, beginning with that of most consequence, and proceeding in order to the most insignificant; each under its generic head, such as the different kinds of grain under corn, and the pulses in the same way. We will place the cereals and pulses of Spain in their order, as an example. First would come wheat, next barley, next beans, next millet. In the same way when they recorded the quantity of arms. First they placed those that were considered most noble, such as lances, next darts, next bows and arrows, then shields, then axes, and then slings. In enumerating the vassals they first gave the account of the natives of each village, and next of those of the whole province combined. On the first string they put only men of sixty and upwards, on the second those of fifty, on the third those of forty, and so on down to the babies at the breast. The women were counted in the same order.

Some of these strings had other finer ones of the same colour attached to them, to serve as supplements or exceptions to the chief record. Thus, if the main string of men of a certain age had reference to the married people, the supplementary string gave the number of widowers of the same age in that year. For these accounts were made up annually, and only related to one year. The knots indicated units, tens, hundreds, thousands, and tens of thousands, but they rarely or never went beyond that; because each village was taken by itself, and each district, and neither ever reached to a number beyond tens of thousands, though there were plenty within that limit. But if it was necessary to record a number equal to hundreds of thousands, they could do it, for in their language they were able to express any number known in arithmetic; but as they had no occasion to go beyond tens of thousands, they did not use higher numbers. These numbers were counted by knots made on the threads, each number being divided from the next. But the knots for each number were made together in one company, like the knots represented on the girdle of the ever blessed Patriarch St. Francis; and this could easily be done as there were never more than nine, seeing that the units, tens, etc., do not exceed that number. On the uppermost knot they put the highest number, which was the tens of thousands, on the next below the thousands, and so on to the units. The knots of each number, and each thread, were placed in a line with each other, exactly in the way a good accountant places his figures to make a long addition sum. These knots or *Quipus* were in charge of Indians who

were called *Quipucamayu*, which means "He who has charge of the accounts." Although there was, at that time, little difference of character among the Indians, because owing to their gentle dispositions and excellent government all might be called good, yet the best, and those who had given the longest proofs of their fitness, were selected for these and other offices. They were not given away from motives of favouritism, because these Indians were never influenced by such considerations, but from considerations of special fitness. Nor were these either sold or farmed out, for they knew nothing of renting, buying, or selling, having no money. They exchanged one article of food for another, and no more; for they neither sold clothes, nor houses, nor estates.

The *Quipucamayus* being so trustworthy and honest, as we have described, their number was regulated according to the population in each village; for, however small the village might be, there were four accountants in it, and from that number up to twenty or thirty; though all used the same register. Thus, as only one account was kept, one accountant would have been sufficient; but the Incas desired that there should be several in each village to act as checks upon each other, and they said that where there were many all must be in fault or none....

The Inca Pachacutec Increased the Number of Schools and Regulated Their Administration

The Father Blas Valera, speaking of this Inca, says as follows: "The Inca Huiraccocha being dead and worshipped among the Indians as a god, his son, the great Titu, with surname of Manco Capac, succeeded him. This was his name until his father gave him that of

A portrait of Manco Capac, first Inca and founder of the dynasty.

Pachacutec, which means 'Reformer of the World.' That title was confirmed afterwards by his distinguished acts and sayings, insomuch that his first name was entirely forgotten. He governed his empire with so much industry, prudence and resolution, as well in peace as in war, that not only did he increase the boundaries of all the four quarters, called *Ttahua-ntin-suyu*, but also he enacted many laws, all which have been confirmed by our Catholic kings, except those relating to idolatry and to forbidden degrees of marriage. This Inca above all things ennobled and increased, with great privileges, the schools that were founded in Cuzco by the King Inca Rocca. He added to the number of the masters, and ordered that all the lords of vassals and captains and their sons, and all the Indians who held any office, should speak the language of Cuzco; and that no one should receive any office or lordship who was not well acquainted with it. In order that this useful law might have full effect, he appointed very

learned masters for the sons of the princes and nobles, not only for those in Cuzco, but also for those throughout the provinces, in which he stationed masters that they might teach the language of Cuzco to all who were employed in the service of the state. Thus it was that in the whole empire of Peru one language was spoken, although now (owing to negligence) many provinces, where it was once understood, have entirely lost it, not without great injury to the preaching of the gospel. All the Indians who, by obeying this law, still retain a knowledge of the language of Cuzco, are more civilized and more intelligent than the others.

"This Pachacutec prohibited any one, except princes and their sons, from wearing gold, silver, precious stones, plumes of feathers of different colours, nor the wool of the vicuña, which they weave with admirable skill. He permitted the people to be moderately ornamented on the first days of the month, and on some other festivals...."

Other Laws of the Inca Pachacutec

"In fine this King, with the advice of his Council, made many laws, rules, ordinances, and customs for the good of the people in numerous provinces. He also abolished many others which were detrimental either to the public peace or to his sovereignty. He also enacted many statutes against blasphemy, patricide, fratricide, homicide, treason, adultery, child-stealing, seduction, theft, arson; as well as regulations for the ceremonies of the temple. He confirmed many more that had been enacted by the Incas his ancestors; such as that sons should obey and serve their fathers until they reached the age of twenty-five, that none should marry without the consent of the parents, and of the parents of the girl;

The teaching methods of the evangelists depicted by Felipe Guamán Poma de Ayala.

that a marriage without this consent was invalid and the children illegitimate; but that if the consent was obtained afterwards the children then became legitimate. This Inca also confirmed the laws of inheritance to lordships according to the ancient customs of each province; and he forbade the judges from receiving bribes from litigants. This Inca made many other laws of less importance, which I omit, to avoid prolixity. Further on I shall relate what laws he made for the guidance of judges, for the contracting of marriages, for making wills, and for the army, as well as for reckoning the years. In our time the

Viceroy, Don Francisco de Toledo, changed or revoked many laws and regulations made by this Inca; and the Indians, admiring his absolute power, called him the second Pachacutec, for they said he was the Reformer of the first Reformer. Their reverence and veneration for this Inca was so great that to this day they cannot forget him."

Down to this point is from what I found amongst the torn papers of Father Blas Valera. That which he promises to write further on, touching the judges, marriages, wills, the army, and the reckoning of the year, is lost, which is a great pity....

Of the Precious Leaf Called *Cuca*, and of Tobacco

It would not be reasonable to forget the plant which the Indians call *cuca* and the Spaniards *coca*. This plant has been and is the principal wealth of Peru, for those who are engaged in trade. It is, therefore, right to give a complete account of it, seeing that it is esteemed so highly by the Indians for its many and great virtues known to them in old times, and for many more which the Spaniards have discovered, in regard to its medicinal uses. The Father Blas Valera, as a close observer, and one who resided many years in Peru and left it more than thirty years after my departure, writes of both the one and the other class of virtues, as one who had tried them. I will first give what his Paternity says, and then add the little that remains to be told. He says:

"The *cuca* is a small bush of the height and thickness of a vine. It has few branches, and on them many delicate leaves of the width of the thumb, and as long as half a thumb's length. They are of a pleasant smell, but not soft. These leaves are called *cuca*, both by Indians

and Spaniards. The Indians are so fond of the *cuca* that they prefer it to gold, silver, and precious stones. They cultivate it with great care and diligence, and are even more careful in getting in the crop. They pick the leaves, one by one, by hand, and dry them in the sun. But they do not swallow the leaves. They merely enjoy the flavour, and pass out the juice. It may be gathered how powerful the *cuca* is, in its effect on the labourers, from the fact that the Indians who use it become stronger and much more satisfied, and work all day without eating. The *cuca* preserves the body from many infirmities, and our doctors use it pounded, for applications to sores and broken bones, to remove cold from the body, or to prevent it from entering, as well as to cure sores that are full of maggots. If it is so beneficial and has such singular virtue in the cure of outward sores, it will surely have even more virtue and efficacy in the entrails of those who eat it? It has another important use, which is that the greater part of the revenue of the bishops and canons of the cathedral of Cuzco is derived from the tithe of the *cuca* leaves; and they enrich many Spaniards who trade with them. But some people, ignoring all these virtues, have said and written many things against the little plant, with no other reason than that the gentiles, in ancient times, and now some wizards and diviners, offered *cuca* to the idols, on which ground these people say that its use ought to be entirely prohibited...."

Thus far is from Blas Valera. To add a few more particulars, we will first remark that these little plants are about the height of a man, and, in planting them, they put the seeds into nurseries, in the same way as with garden stuffs, but drilling a hole as for vines. They layer the plants as with a vine. They take the

C oca is still transported in bundles of dried leaves.

greatest care that no roots, not even the smallest, be doubled, for this is sufficient to make the plant dry up. When they gather the leaves, they take each branch within the fingers of the hand, and pick the leaves until they come to the final sprout, which they do not touch, lest it should cause the branch to wither. The leaf, both on the upper and under side, in shape and greenness, is neither more nor less than that of the arbutus [a plant of the heath family], except that three or four leaves of the *cuca*, being very delicate, would make one of an arbutus in thickness. I rejoice to be able to find things in Spain which are appropriate for comparison with those of that country, that both here and there people may know one by another. After the leaves are gathered, they put them in the sun to dry. For they lose their green colour, which is much prized, and break up into powder, being so very delicate, if they are exposed to damp in the *cestos* or baskets in which they are carried from one place to another. The baskets are made of split canes, of which there are

many of all sizes in these provinces of the Andes. They cover the outside of the baskets with the leaves of the large cane, which are more than a *tercia* wide, and about half a *vara* long, in order to preserve the *cuca* from the wet; for the leaves are much injured by damp. The basket is then enveloped by an outer net made of a certain fibre. In considering the number of things that are required for the production of *cuca*, it would be more profitable to return thanks to God for providing all things in the places where they are necessary, than to write concerning them, for the account must seem incredible. They gather the *cuca* leaves every four months, which makes three harvests a year. If the ground is weeded well and thoroughly of the numerous herbs that continually spring up, by reason of the warmth and dampness of the climate, each harvest may be anticipated by more than a fortnight, which makes nearly four harvests in the year....

Of the plant which the Spaniards call tobacco, and the Indians *sayri*, we shall speak in the other part. Doctor Monardo writes wonders concerning it. The *sarsaparilla* needs no praise from anyone; for its own deeds are its sufficient praise, both in the Old World and the New, in curing bubos [swelling in a lymph gland] and other grave infirmities. There are many other herbs in Peru of such virtue as medicines that, as Father Blas Valera says, if they were all known it would be unnecessary to bring any from Spain, or from anywhere else. But the Spanish doctors think so little of them, that even those that were formerly known to the Indians, are, for the most part, forgotten.

Garcilaso de la Vega
Royal Commentaries of the Incas (1609)
Translated by Clements R. Markham
1869–71

Rites and Religion in the Old World

The Inca calendar was punctuated by a series of festivals. Most of these either celebrated major events in the agricultural cycle—sowing, the first rains, or harvest— or corresponded with various points in the astronomical calendar, such as the solstices or equinoxes.

A native band playing drums and panpipes.

The following extract comes from The Fables and Rites of the Incas *by Cristobal de Molina, published in 1573. The work is an important one, for Molina had a good understanding of the Quechua language and was thus able to learn of Inca religious practices before the conquest from native chiefs and other important people in the community. Here he describes the festival of the Situa (La Citua), which took place in August.*

The month of August was called Coya-raymi; and in it they celebrated the *Situa*. In order to perform the ceremonies of this festival, they brought the figures of their *huacas* from all parts of the land, from Quito to Chile, and placed them in the houses they had in Cuzco, for the purpose which we shall presently explain. The reason for celebrating the feast called *Situa*, in this month, was, because the rains commenced, and with the first rains there was generally much sickness. They besought the Creator that, during the year, he would be pleased to shield them from sickness, as well as in Cuzco, as throughout the territory conquered by the Incas. On the day of the conjunction of the moon, at noon the Inca, with all the chiefs of his council, and the other principal lords who were in Cuzco, went to the Coricancha, which is the house and temple of the Sun, where they agreed together on the way in which the festival should be celebrated; for in one year they added, and in another they reduced the number of ceremonies, according to circumstances.

All things having been arranged, the High Priest addressed the assembly, and said that the ceremonies of the *Situa* should be performed, that the Creator might drive all the diseases and evils from the land. A great number of armed men, accoutred for war, with their lances, then came to the square in front of the temple. The figures called *Chuquilla* and *Uiracocha* were brought to the temple of the Sun from their own special temples.…The priests of these *huacas* joined the assembly, and, with the concurrence of all present, the priest of the Sun proclaimed the feast. First, all strangers, all whose ears were broken, and all deformed persons were sent out of the city, it being said that they should take no part in the ceremony, because they were in that state as a punishment for some fault. Unfortunate people ought not to be present, it was believed, because their ill-luck might drive away some piece of good fortune. They also drove out the dogs, that they might not howl. Then the people, who were armed as if for war, went to the square of Cuzco, crying out: "O sicknesses, disasters, misfortunes, and dangers, go forth from the land." In the middle of the square, where stood the urn of gold which was like a fountain, that was used at the sacrifice of *chicha*, four hundred men of war assembled. One hundred faced towards Colla-suyu, which is the direction of the Sun-rising. One hundred faced to the westward, which is the direction of Chinchasuyu. Another hundred looked towards Antisuyu, which is the north, and the last hundred turned towards the south. They had with them all the arms that are used in their wars. As soon as those who came from the temple of the Sun arrived in the square, they cried out and said: "Go forth all evils." The people of Huvin-Cuzco carried these cries, and there they delivered them over to the *mitimaes* of Huayparya, who in their turn passed them to the *mitimaes* of Atahuaylla, and

Inca warriors exorcising evil spirits.

thus they were passed to the *mitimaes* of Huaray-pacha, who continued them as far as the river at Quiquisana, where they bathed themselves and their arms. Thus was the shouting ended in that direction.…

Such was the ceremony for driving the sicknesses out of Cuzco. Their reason for bathing in these rivers was because they were rivers of great volume, and were supposed to empty themselves into the sea, and to carry the evils with them. When the ceremony commenced in Cuzco, all the people, great and small, came to their doors, crying out, shaking their mantles and *llicllas*, and shouting, "Let the evils be gone. How greatly desired has this festival been by us. O creator of all things, permit us to reach another year, that we may see another feast like this." They all danced,

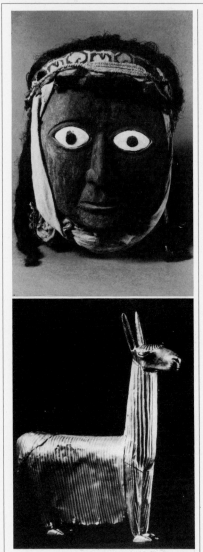

A funerary mask with inlays (top) and a silver statuette used during rites held to assure the fertility of llamas (above).

including the Inca, and in the morning twilight they went to the rivers and fountains to bathe, saying that their maladies would come out of them. Having finished bathing, they took great torches of straw, bound round with cords, which they lighted and continued to play with them, passing them from one to the other. They called these torches of straw *pancurcu*. At the end of their feast they returned to their houses, and by that time a pudding of coarsely ground maize had been prepared, called *sancu* and *elbu*. This they applied to their faces, to the lintels of their doors, and to the places where they kept their food and clothes. Then they took the *sancu* to the fountains, and threw it in, saying, "May we be free from sickness, and may no maladies enter this house." They also sent this *sancu* to their relations and friends for the same purpose, and they put it on the bodies of their dead that they also might enjoy the benefits of the feast. Afterwards the women ate and drank their food with much enjoyment; and on this day each person, how poor soever he might be, was to eat and drink, for they said that on this day they should enjoy themselves, if they had to pass all the rest of the year in labour and sorrow. On this day no man scolded his neighbour, nor did any word pass in anger, nor did anyone claim what was owing to him from another. They said that there would be trouble and strife throughout the year, if any was commenced on the day of the festival.

In the night, the statues of the Sun, of the Creator, and of the Thunder, were brought out, and the priests of each of these statues warmed it with the before mentioned *sancu*. In the morning they brought the best food they could prepare to present at the temples of the Creator, of the Sun, and of the Thunder; which the priests of those *huacas* received and consumed. They also brought out the bodies of the dead lords and ladies which were embalmed, each one being brought out by the person of the same lineage who had charge of it. During the night these bodies were washed in the baths which belonged to them when they were alive. They were then brought back to their houses, and warmed with the same coarse pudding called *çancu* [*sic*]; and the food they had been most fond of when they were alive was placed before them, and afterwards the persons who were in charge of the bodies consumed the food.

The persons who had charge of the *huaca* called *Guana-caucique*, which is a great figure of a man, washed it and warmed it with the *sancu*; and the principal Inca lord and his wife, after they had finished their bath, put the same *sancu* in their house, and on their hands. Afterwards, they placed certain plumes on their heads, of a bird called *pialco*, which are of a changing colour. The same was done with the figure of the Creator, and those who had charge of it called this ceremony *Pilcoyacu*. At about eight or nine in the morning the principal lord Inca, with his wife, and the lords of the council who were in his house, came forth into the great square of Cuzco, richly dressed. They also brought out the image of the Sun called *Apupunchau*, which was the principal image among those in the temple. They were accompanied by all the priests of the Sun, who brought the two figures of

Surrounded by members of the nobility, the Great Inca offers the sacred drink *chicha* (maize beer) to his ancestor the sun.

gold, and their women called Inca-Ollo and Palla-Ollo. There also came forth the woman called Coya-facssa, who was dedicated to the Sun. She was either the sister or the daughter of the ruler. The priests carried the image of the Sun, and placed it on a bench prepared for it in the square. The priests of the Creator likewise brought forth his image, and deposited it in its place. So also did the priests of the Thunder, called Chuquiylla, bring forth his image. Each had its bench of gold, and before them were borne *yauris*, which were made like sceptres of gold. The priests of these *huacas* came in very rich dresses, to celebrate this feast. Those who had charge of the *huaca* called Huanacauri, also brought its figure into the square. They say that a woman was never assigned to the *huaca* of the Creator. It was believed that the Creator did not need women, because, as he created them, they all belonged to him. In all their sacrifices, the first was offered to the Creator. At this feast they brought out all the embalmed bodies of their lords and ladies, very richly adorned. The bodies were carried by the descendants of the respective lineages, and were deposited in the square on seats of gold, according to the order in which they lived.

All the people of Cuzco came out, according to their tribes and lineages, as richly dressed as their means would allow; and, having made reverences to the Creator, the Sun, and the lord Inca, they sat down on their benches [and] passed the day in eating and drinking, and enjoying themselves; and they performed the *tauqui* called *alançitua saqui*, in red shirts down to their feet, and garlands called *pilco-casa* on their heads; accompanied with large or small tubes of canes, which made a kind of

music called *tica-tica*. They gave thanks to the Creator for having spared them to see that day, and prayed that they might pass another year without sickness; and they did the same to the Sun and to the Thunder. The Inca came with them, having the Sun before him. He had a great vase of gold containing *chicha*. It was received by the priest, who emptied it into the urn, which, as has been said, is like a stone fountain plated with gold. This urn had a hole made in such a way, that the *chicha* could enter a pipe or sewer passing under the ground to the houses of the Sun, the Thunder, and the Creator.

The next day they all came to the great square in the same order, placing the *huacas* on their benches as before. The Inca and the people brought with them a very great quantity of flocks.… The number of animals was so great, according to those who made this declaration, that they amounted to more than one hundred thousand, and it was necessary that all should be without spot or blemish, and with fleeces that had never been shorn. Presently the priest of the Sun selected four of the most perfect, and sacrificed them in the following order: one was offered to the Creator, another to the Thunder, another to the Sun, and another to Huanacauri. When this sacrifice was offered up, the priest had the *sancu* on great plates of gold, and he sprinkled it with the blood of the sheep. The high priest then said in a loud voice so that all might hear: "Take heed how you eat this *sancu*; for he who eats it in sin, and with a double will and heart, is seen by our father, the Sun, who will punish him with grievous troubles. But he who with a single heart partakes of it, to him the Sun and the Thunder will show favour, and will grant children and happy years, and abundance, and all that he requires." Then they all rose up to partake, first making a solemn vow before eating the *yahuar-sancu*, in which they promised never to murmur against the Creator, the Sun, or the Thunder; never to be traitors to their lord the Inca, on pain of receiving condemnation and trouble. The priest of the Sun then took what he could hold on three fingers, put it into his mouth, and returned to his seat. In this order, and in this manner of taking the oath, all the tribes rose up, and thus all partook down to the little children. They all kept some of the *yahuar-sancu* for those who were absent, and sent some to those who were confined to their beds by sickness; for they believed it to be very unlucky for any one not to partake of the *yahuar-sancu* on that day. They took it with such care that no particle was allowed to fall to the ground, this being looked upon as a great sin. When they killed the sacrificial sheep, they took out the lungs and inflated them, and the priests judged, from certain signs on them, whether all things would turn out prosperously in the coming year or not. Afterwards, they burnt them before the Creator, the Sun, and the Thunder. The bodies of the sheep were divided and distributed, as very sacred things, a very small piece to each person. The rest was given to the people of Cuzco to eat, and each man, as he entered the square, pulled off a piece of the wool, with which he sacrificed to the Sun.

Cristobal de Molina
The Fables and Rites of the Incas (1573)
Translated by Clements R. Markham
1873

Sacrifice of a black llama on the day of Inti Rami, the festival of the sun.

"Archaeologist Wants to Reconquer Shrine for Incas"

After the death of the last Inca, many traditional rites lost their relevance. And yet the Catholicism that developed in Peru was founded in more ways than one on the ancient Inca rituals.

CON3EDERACION
COMOHI3ODIOSCIELO

A drawing by Felipe Guamán Poma de Ayala showing the Christian god holding aloft the deified heavenly bodies of the Incas.

The history of post-conquest Peru is in many ways typified by the struggles between the Catholic church and traditional Andean culture. Nowhere is this more apparent than at the monastery of Santo Domingo in Cuzco, where a colonial church sits atop one of the most important Inca buildings, the temple of the sun known as Coricancha (or Koricancha). As this newspaper report reveals, archaeologists eager to investigate the Inca structure face serious opposition from the Catholic priests.

CUZCO, Peru—Raymundo Béjar Navarro, an archeologist, climbs the adobe wall up onto the grounds of the Santo Domingo monastery here in the center of town.

Shaking his head, he complains that the four resident monks are refusing to let his scientific team dig in the area. Defiantly, looking up at the towering, 350-year-old Spanish church, he hisses through his teeth, "They should tear this down."

The reason for such emotion is that the Santo Domingo church and monastery sit atop the holiest shrine of the Inca culture—the Temple of the Sun, or Koricancha in Quechua. And Mr. Béjar is leading a three-year effort to restore the temple.

Two Conflicting Cultures

The church is indeed a mixture of the two conflicting cultures. Its foundations and supporting walls are of the exquisitely carved Inca stones, made out of andesite, that were carved with stone tools from quarries miles away, and so finely shaped at the building site that no mortar was needed. Even today, a knife does not fit between the joints.

Above the Inca masonry is the Spanish construction of roughly cut

A fanciful reconstruction of the temple of the sun, Coricancha, at Cuzco.

stones put together with adobe mortar, giving the church a two-tone texture. Inside, large parts of the gilded baroque monastery have been removed to reveal four stone chambers of the original Inca temple.

Recently the digging has produced a new phase of the centuries-old struggle between the conquerors and the conquered of Peru, between the modern-day Roman Catholic Church and the descendants of the Incas, who yielded to Francisco Pizarro in 1532.

"They have so many churches throughout Peru," Mr. Béjar said. "Why do they have to have one right on top of the holiest Inca site? I thought this was the year when the church was apologizing for past abuses. If they abused anyone, they abused the Incas."

Mr. Béjar, who is a Roman Catholic, has beliefs that have not sat well with the church hierarchy. His thinking has been called blasphemy, and he has received threats of excommunication. Lawsuits have been filed by the Dominican monastery against the city of Cuzco to prevent any "robbing of church property."

"The capricious Mr. Béjar is pretending to take down a church that has been declared a world monument by UNESCO," said the Rev. Domingo Gamarra, director of the monastery. "The church represents the meeting of two cultures. What he is doing is anti-Christian, and we will defend the church to the very end."

Until conquered by the Spanish, the Temple of the Sun was the center of the vast Inca empire that stretched from northern Venezuela to Patagonia in southern Argentina. Here was the repository of the realm's gold treasure, showcase of its exquisite stone carving technology and central seat of government.

As was customary when the Spaniards conquered an area, they imposed Catholicism on the Incas and used the

Koricancha structure as a church. In 1650 an earthquake destroyed part of the temple, so the Spanish tore most of the temple down and used the finely cut stones to build the existing church and monastery.

In 1953 another quake hit the building. Many of the Spanish-built walls collapsed, revealing parts of the original structure hidden for centuries. In reconstructing Santo Domingo, church officials agreed not to build on some of the existing Inca walls.

For Jesus Cheque, a Quechua Indian working on the digging project, the idea of the Santo Domingo church resting atop the Inca temple is a bitter one, and he says flatly that he wants the church torn down.

"It's the symbol of the oppression of our culture, the abuse of my Andean past," he said. "Where is my place to worship? They have stolen the stones of my temple."

Such cultural sensitivities are being fed by politicians. Daniel Estrada, Mayor of Cuzco, in his third term, has been highly successful, appealing to the Inca roots of Cuzqueños, as Cuzco residents are known.

Mayor Pledges Sensitivity

"This is a victimized society, oppressed and suppressed for centuries, and we intend to change that by being sensitive to the Andean beliefs," Mr. Estrada said. "For them Cuzco is the Sacred City."

Recently, Mr. Estrada has invested money earned from taxes on soft drinks and other items to rejuvenate Cuzco, installing fountains, rebuilding narrow streets in the old part of town and putting up a 40-foot statue of the great Inca emperor, Pachacutec, on top of a 110-foot stone base, at a cost of more than $1 million.

But Koricancha represents his most ambitious project. Using $2 million of the municipality's funds, the Mayor bought the land around the temple, tore down the existing houses and began excavating in the area that once was the outer court.

But motives to resurrect the Inca culture have a mercantile side as well. The Inca ruins around Cuzco, including the breathtaking Machu Picchu, have created Peru's tourist engine. But problems with guerrilla violence and cholera in early 1991 cut tourism down to 15 percent of its levels in the early 1980s. This has left 40 percent of Cuzqueños unemployed and 20 percent underemployed.

Slight Recovery in Tourism

Tourism has seen a slight recovery in the two and a half years since the outbreak of cholera in early 1991, but only to 40 percent of previous levels.

A restored Koricancha is considered to be a major piece in reviving tourism in Cuzco. But if the dispute is not resolved, it may look like just nondescript ruins next to a colonial church. And, what's more, the most scientifically important site of Koricancha—the central temple chamber—may never be touched by archeologists, since it rests directly under the church's sanctuary.

"The monks don't want to let anyone dig, because they are afraid they'll lose the property," said Professor John Rowe, an archeologist at the University of California in Berkeley and an adviser to the Koricancha project. "They are only a few monks in a huge piece of property, but no one here wants to take on the church."

Nathaniel C. Nash
The New York Times
31 August 1993

The Catholic church of Santo Domingo, built on the foundations of Coricancha—the temple of the sun at Cuzco.

When Two Worlds Collide

The Spanish conquest brought about a veritable revolution in the New World: a demographic collapse due to the introduction of new diseases, a mingling of populations, and an ecological upheaval through the arrival of European animals and plants. Brutally, the Old World invaded the New.

The Disease Factor

The huge epidemics that wiped out nine-tenths of the indigenous populations of Peru and Bolivia is a factor that tends to be overlooked in the dramatic story of the conquest. But besides affecting the numerical strength of the native peoples, it struck lethally at the survivors' will to resist.

All these factors conspired to make Amerindian populations radically vulnerable to the disease organisms Spaniards and, before long, also Africans, brought with them across the ocean. The magnitude of the resultant disaster has only recently become clear. Learned opinion before World War II systematically underestimated Amerindian populations, putting the total somewhere between eight and fourteen million at the time Columbus landed in Hispaniola. Recent estimates, however, based on sampling of tribute lists, missionary reports and elaborate statistical arguments, have multiplied such earlier estimates tenfold and more, putting Amerindian population on the eve of the conquest at about one hundred million, with twenty-five to thirty million of this total assignable to the Mexican and an approximately equal number to the Andean civilizations. Relatively dense populations also apparently existed in the connecting Central American lands.

Starting from such levels, population decay was catastrophic. By 1568, less than fifty years from the time Cortez inaugurated epidemiological as well as other exchanges between Amerindians and European populations, the population of central Mexico had

Dance of the natives of Lima.

shrunk to about three million, i.e., to about one tenth of what had been there when Cortez landed. Decay continued, though at a reduced rate, for another fifty years, reaching a low point of about 1.6 million by 1620. Recovery did not definitely set in for another thirty years or so and remained very slow until the eighteenth century.

Similarly drastic destruction of pre-existing Amerindian societies also occurred in other parts of the Americas, continuing even into the twentieth century. Disaster is to be expected whenever some previously remote and isolated tribe comes into contact with the outside world and there encounters a series of destructive and demoralizing epidemics. A relatively recent case history will illustrate how ruthless and seemingly irresistible such a process can be. In 1903 a South American tribe, the Cayapo, accepted a missionary—a single priest—who bent every effort to safeguard his flock from the evils and dangers of civilization. When he arrived the tribe was between six thousand and eight thousand strong, yet only five hundred survived in 1918. By 1927 only twenty-seven were alive and in 1950 two or three individuals tracing descent to the Cayapo still existed, but the tribe had totally disappeared—and this despite the best intentions and a deliberate attempt to shield the Indians from disease as well as other risks of outside contacts....

Clearly, if smallpox had not come when it did, the Spanish victory could not have been achieved in Mexico. The same was true of Pizarro's filibuster into Peru. For the smallpox epidemic in Mexico did not confine its ravages to Aztec territory. Instead, it spread to Guatemala, where it appeared in 1520, and continued southward, penetrating

Burial rites for an important member of the Inca community.

the Inca domain in 1525 or 1526. Consequences there were just as dramatic as among the Aztecs. The reigning Inca died of the disease while away from his capital on campaign in the North. His designated heir also died, leaving no legitimate successor. Civil war ensued, and it was amid this wreckage of the Inca political structure that Pizarro and his crew of roughnecks made their way to Cuzco and plundered its treasures. He met no serious military resistance at all.

Two points seem particularly worth emphasizing here. First, Spaniards and Indians readily agreed that epidemic disease was a particularly dreadful and unambiguous form of divine punishment. Interpretation of pestilence as a sign of God's displeasure was a part of the Spanish inheritance, enshrined in the Old Testament and in the whole Christian tradition. The Amerindians, lacking all experience of anything remotely like the initial series of lethal epidemics, concurred. Their religious doctrines recognized that superhuman power lodged in deities whose behaviour towards men was often angry. It was natural, therefore, for them to assign an unexampled effect to a supernatural cause, quite apart from the Spanish missionary efforts that urged the same interpretation of the catastrophe upon dazed and demoralized converts.

Secondly, the Spaniards were nearly immune from the terrible disease that raged so mercilessly among the Indians. They had almost always been exposed in childhood and so developed effective immunity. Given the interpretation of the cause of pestilence accepted by both parties, such a manifestation of divine partiality for the invaders was conclusive. The gods of the Aztecs as much as the God of the Christians seemed to agree that the white newcomers had divine approval for all they did. And while God thus seemed to favour the whites, regardless of their morality and piety or lack thereof, his wrath was visited upon the Indians with an unrelenting harshness that often puzzled and distressed the Christian missionaries who soon took charge of the moral and religious life of their converts along the frontiers of Spain's American dominions.

From the Amerindian point of view, stunned acquiescence in Spanish superiority was the only possible response. No matter how few their numbers or how brutal and squalid their behaviour, the Spaniards prevailed. Native authority structures crumbled; the old gods seemed to have abdicated. The situation was ripe for the mass conversions recorded so proudly by Christian missionaries. Docility to the commands of priests, viceroys, landowners, mining entrepreneurs, tax collectors, and anyone else who spoke with a loud voice and had a white skin was another inevitable consequence. When the divine and natural orders were both unambiguous in declaring against native tradition and belief, what ground for resistance remained? The extraordinary ease of Spanish conquests and the success a few hundred men had in securing control of vast areas and millions of persons is unintelligible on any other basis.

William H. McNeill
Plagues and Peoples, 1976

Ethnic Minorities

In 1988 a group of Latin American political leaders asked Oxford Analytica, an international business and government consulting firm based at Oxford University, to make an objective appraisal of the social, political, and economic problems facing Latin America today.

Since the last century, the "modernizing" instinct has led Latin American governments to try to integrate their ethnic minorities economically, socially, and even politically. In schools, members of ethnic groups have long been encouraged to believe in the virtues of republican democracy. Policies to modernize agriculture and to integrate peasants into a national economy also sought to incorporate ethnic groups into the "national" society. But despite this, social stratification has generally continued to reflect ethnic origins, exposing the myth of racial democracy. Encouragement of ethnic groups, by the state or by intellectuals, to stand up for their own cultural identities and values also has a long history.

However, increasingly there are many signs of ethnic groups themselves beginning to revindicate their "nationhoods" and champion the rights of the so-called Fourth World, often vigorously supported by vocal pressure groups in the First World.... At the same time, though, that degree of ethnic self-consciousness may prove to be transitory since, with the drift of members of ethnic groups from a rural to an urban society, the symbols of ethnic identity may become more a folkloric memory than live patterns of belief.

From spread of disease, disruption of settlement patterns, physical extermination, and forced labor by the Spaniards and others, the population of native Amerindians fell dramatically from the time of the conquest onward. The areas where indigenous peoples persisted in largest numbers, where their cultures and language endured, or where indigenous societies proved particularly strong and resilient, were either remote or difficult to conquer. These areas are still where most ethnic Amerindians, the direct descendants of pre-Columbian cultures, live today.

The calculation of numbers cannot be at all precise. In the literature on ethnicity no two writers use exactly the same criteria to define ethnic identity. The most recent and comprehensive analysis of the demography of indigenous peoples yields the following figures. The total indigenous population in the whole hemisphere—North and South America—was around 28.5 million people in 1978. Of these 27.9 million were in Latin America, approximately 6.5 percent of Latin America's total population. A previous estimate published in 1962 for the whole of the hemisphere put the indigenous population at just over 13 million. Even discounting inaccuracies and discrepancies in methods used to measure population, it is clear that indigenous populations are not falling. Given these estimates, they appear to have more than doubled in a period of sixteen years.

The highland Indian communities of Latin American have undergone very significant changes as a result of their progressive incorporation into the national economy. The effects of migration to the cities and the tendency for traditional communal forms of production to disappear, especially in

An 18th-century artist painted a series of portraits illustrating the racial hierarchy imposed on Peruvians at the time. Included were portraits of a child of a Spanish colonist and a black African (left), then referred to as a *mulatto,* and the child of a colonist and a *mulatta* (right), referred to as a *morisco.*

areas like highland Peru where they have traditionally been very important, are often taken as signs that ethnic consciousness is being diluted. Migration supposedly signifies a rupture between rural life and urban life. In most cases no such rupture exists, partly because in many cases migration is not permanent, and even when it is, those who migrate maintain links with their former communities, moving back and forth between their urban and rural spheres. This movement helps explain the proliferation of bus companies in many Latin American countries.

Another reason for the absence of a sudden rupture is that consciousness of ethnicity persists in the urban environment, although the cultural forms it takes may change. Peru is the country with the largest concentration of indigenous people in urban areas. About 30 percent of the total indigenous population now live in cities, mainly in Lima, where the new cultural expressions of ethnicity are to be found that represent a fusion of Andean-rural with coastal-urban forms. "Chicha" music is but one. In Guatemala and Bolivia 25 percent of all indigenous people live in cities, and in Mexico and Ecuador the proportion is about 10 percent.

In Peru two specific influences have combined to further alter the pattern of rural life in the highlands: the growth in coca cultivation; and the impact of the Sendero Luminoso (Shining Path) guerrilla organization.

The massive expansion of coca cultivation in the 1980s in response to world demand for cocaine has been concentrated in [Peru and Bolivia]…. Because of the profitability of coca farming…and because the crop requires a substantial labor force, coca farming has a strong attraction for people from all over the highlands in both countries. Though some may have been able to acquire land, the majority are wage laborers. Both in terms of the corruption and violence cocaine engenders and in terms of dedication of land to coca rather than food, the growth of narco-agriculture and drug trafficking has had a disturbing influence in rural areas where coca is grown.

Sendero Luminoso, Peru's messianic guerrilla movement, has also had a disturbing influence, especially in the southern and central sierra, where it has been most persistently active. Most victims of the conflict between Sendero and the security forces have been innocent peasants whose loyalty each side tries to win. Depopulation has resulted from migration within the sierra area, from rural communities to provincial towns and to big cities.

Ethnicity undoubtedly plays an important part in defining the characteristics of peasant movements and rural tensions. Indeed, strong ethnic identity is one of the conditions that favors guerrilla warfare. Sendero Luminoso, despite its dogmatic Maoist rhetoric, has a keen sense of the customs and beliefs of Quechua-speaking Indians, whereas the orthodox Peruvian left has always had difficulty in subordinating class to ethnic concepts. In Bolivia, by contrast, the strength of *indigenismo* [a doctrine advocating pride in native culture and values] in peasant unions owes much to a successful blend of class and racial consciousness. In countries like Bolivia and Peru, and to a lesser extent in Ecuador, Colombia, and Mexico, ethnicity will continue to be an important element in rural politics.

Oxford Analytica
Latin America in Perspective
1991

Swords or Plowshares?

The Spaniards deliberately did not plant olive trees in their colonies in the Americas because Spain wanted to keep its commercial monopoly in olive oil.

Many places in this kingdom, such as the coast valleys and the land on the banks of rivers, are very fertile, and yield wheat, maize, and barley in great quantities. There are also not a few vineyards at San Miguel, Truxillo, the City of the Kings, Cuzco, and Guamanga, and they are beginning to plant them in other parts, so that there is great hope of profitable vine cultivation. There are orange and pomegranate trees, and other trees brought from Spain, besides those of the country; and pulses of all sorts.

In short, Peru is a grand country, and hereafter it will be still greater, for large cities have been founded, and when our age has passed away, Peru may send to other countries wheat, meat, wool, and even silk, for there are the best situations in the world for planting mulberries. There is only one thing that has not yet been brought to this country, and that is the olive tree, which, after bread and the vine, is the most important product. It seems to me that if young plants were brought from Spain, and planted in the coast valleys, and on the banks of rivers in the mountains, there would soon be as large olive woods as there are at Axarafe de Sevilla. For if they require a warm climate it is here; if they want much water, or none, or little, all these requirements can be found here. In some places in Peru it never thunders, lightning is not seen, nor do snows fall in the coast valleys, and these are the things which damage the fruit of olive trees. When the trees

Harvesting maize in the month of May. Imperfect ears were used for making *chicha* beer.

are once planted, there will soon come a time when Peru will be as well supplied with oil as with everything else. No woods of oak trees have been found in Peru, but if they were planted in the Collao, in the district of Cuzco, and in other parts, I believe that they would give the same result as olive trees in the coast valleys.

My opinion is that the conquerors and settlers of these parts should not pass their time in fighting battles and matching in chase of each other; but in planting and sowing, which would be much more profitable.

Pedro Cieza de León
Chronicle of Peru (1553)
Translated by Clements R. Markham
1864

I n the 19th century, Peruvian exoticism took on very strange forms, like this Andean woman dressed in Moorish fashion.

Inca Tribute

The tribute system imposed on the natives by the Spaniards was inspired by and modeled after the Incas' own system of tribute. It failed, however, to take into consideration the ideology of reciprocity that had legitimized it under the Inca.

Money played no part in the Inca economy. Nevertheless goods circulated throughout the Empire, albeit in a somewhat limited fashion: in the first place by barter, but above all through the tribute system.

As we have seen, crops varied with altitude and mountain farmers exchanged their produce for that of the lower valleys: we know that a system of complementary production from high and low lands was the basis of a "vertical economy." Thus the people of Chucuito, on Lake Titicaca, bartered llama wool, *charqui* and *chuño* for maize from the Sama and Moquega regions on the coast, and for the coca from Larecaja and Capinota, in the tropical valleys of the interior. In these transactions, considerable distances were covered.

More generally, the circulation of goods throughout the Empire was ensured by the tribute paid to the Inca: either produce from the Inca's lands came directly to Cuzco or the Inca transferred from one region to another goods that had accumulated in his storehouses. But it was a relatively limited circulation; for one thing we must reckon on considerable local consumption; for another, the peasants owed tribute not only to the Inca, but also to the whole hierarchy of the *curacas*.

All males in the communities between the ages of 25 and 50 (and under 25 if married) were taxpayers, i.e. tributaries (*hatunruna*). Essentially the peasants owed their labour, not the produce of the *ayllu* territory. (But the two were linked: according to the principle of reciprocity, obligation to pay tribute was associated with the right to a share of communal land.) All the *curacas*, from the governor of a province to the chieftain of 100 men, were exempt from manual work and therefore from tribute. There was however one special category of tributaries: the artisans. These men (potters, goldsmiths, etc.) owed only the products of their own craft and were free of all other obligations.

Laborers construct the boundaries of the empire.

Tribute paid to the Inca was paralleled by tribute paid to the *curaca*. In practice, the peasants' obligations were of the following three types:

A. *Collective work on the land.* The fields of the Inca and of the *curacas* were productive only if their owners had a work-force at their disposal. This was supplied in the first instance by the whole of the community: *ayllu* members went off together to the Inca's land to tend it communally. Their work was done to the rhythm of songs and dances of a religious character and the occasion had its place in a total integrated view of the world. The same applied to the *curacas*' land. Thus ties of solidarity among members of the *ayllu* were put at the service of the State and of its administrative apparatus. Produce from the Inca's fields was stored in local or

A 17th-century illustration of life in Peru under the rule of the Spaniards.

provincial storehouses. It appears that the *curacas*, or at any rate the more important of them, also had their own storehouses.

B. *Mita,* personal, periodic service. For the army, or for large-scale projects (the building of roads, bridges, temples, etc.) the State recruited a certain number of tributaries according to requirements and for limited periods of time. *Ayllu* members, conforming to the rules of solidarity, tilled the fields of the absent tributaries. The great projects organized by the State excited the admiration of the chroniclers, and historians have long insisted on the importance of the *mita* performed for the Incas. But the *curacas* could also draw on this form of tribute, whether for their domestic needs or for the cultivation of their fields or the guarding of their herds. Thus at Chucuito, Martín Cari had sixty Indians working for him every year and Martín Cusi had thirty. And as in the case of community work, the *mitayos* were both fed and rewarded by Inca or *curaca.*

C. *Textile tribute.* Woven fabrics and clothes played a special role in the Inca State: [archaeologist] J. V. Murra has shown that they had not only economic but also religious and magical significance; they were burnt or buried in sacrifices to the *huacas* and to the gods. When the Spanish arrived, they were astonished at the vast stores of cloth contained in the State depots. In fact every family spun and wove for the Inca its own quota of tribute, which varied with the supplies available. But it is always made clear that the Inca provided the raw material to be worked; the tributaries were not expected to draw on the communal store; here again they owed their labour, no more. For example in the Huánuco region, in the north of the Empire, herds of llamas were few and the farmers grew cotton: but according to the informants of Ortiz de Zúñiga, the communities owed woolen fabrics as tribute, the wool itself being provided by the Inca. The same arrangement operated between peasants and *curacas*: the latter also levied tribute of woven fabrics, providing the raw material themselves. One may wonder whether this tribute was a tax on the whole of the community or only on the *mitayos* doing their annual service for the *curaca.* From what we know of Martín Cari it seems that both possibilities existed.

In short, tribute was an integral part of the system of reciprocity: the peasants tilled the Inca's land in exchange for the right to use community land: similarly, in exchange for the right to draw on the community's wool (or cotton) they wove the Inca's wool. These obligations did not result solely from notions of the universal proprietorial rights of the Inca: he, the son of the Sun, was the source of divine protection for his subjects, he assured the order of society and bestowed favours and rewards. In particular, the Inca's generosity provided for the welfare of those who were old or sick and unable to work. In time of famine, he distributed to the communities the reserve stocks from his granaries. The peasants felt therefore that they shared in the consumption of the produce they delivered as tribute. The *curaca* played a similar role lower down the scale. In fact, duties to the Inca seem to have been an extension of duties to the *curaca*, as though the Empire had established itself by modelling its institutions on those already in

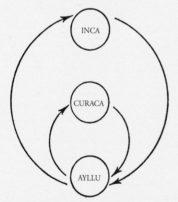

existence. In conclusion, it amounted to a dual system of gifts and counter-gifts as shown in the diagram [above].

This dual system then consisted of central collection of goods by the Inca and their subsequent redistribution to

the Empire.... However, despite the Inca's role, tribute was mainly a local matter. We must not overlook the importance of provincial administration: the greater part of stocks was consumed locally and most of the *mitayos* also served locally. We can therefore understand why the Inca forbade his subjects to leave their communities, except with his express permission: tribute weighed collectively on each *ayllu*, it was levied under the supervision of the *curacas* and consequently required a stable tribute-paying population. Hence a remarkable dialectical process: to some extent tribute enabled goods to circulate throughout the empire, but at the same time it reinforced social immobility. For one thing, the communal system itself assumed a degree of stability: it was founded on patterns of kinship, on the redistribution of land, and the *ayllu* member could scarcely imagine himself breaking the ties of reciprocity which were for him the definition of social life. For another, rotation of the *mita*, collective work on the Inca's land, situated irrevocably in their own territory, bound the tributaries to the *ayllu* of their birth. In conclusion, tribute played a double role: it linked the community to a much greater unit, but at the same time it isolated it in its local setting and consolidated its traditional structures.

Colonial Tribute

The basic problem is: how did the Spanish tribute compare with the Inca tribute? Quantitatively, we lack precise data. However, at Huánuco, Chucuito and Huaura we have witnessed a development of grave consequence: the Spanish appropriated lands belonging to the Inca and the Sun, lands formerly reserved for tribute; as a result, the

View of Chulumani (top), capital of the province of Yungas in Bolivia. Above: Chorrillos man in festival attire (Peru).

burden of tribute was transferred to the communal lands of the Indian people. Often the tax codes themselves, under Gasca as under Toledo, explicitly confirm that the tributaries were to harvest their tribute of maize and wheat from their own fields. It is true that the Indians were less numerous and in general…were not short of land (although they had lost the best); but precisely because they were fewer in number, they had more work to do. It is therefore not surprising that Spanish tribute seemed to them much more burdensome than that of the Inca: the indications we have concerning the amount of time spent in working to pay the *encomenderos'* dues (at Huánuco and at Huaura) seem to point to an intensive exploitation of the Indian population. It would be naive to assume that the tax beneficiaries obeyed the laws to the letter: innumerable documents bear witness to malpractices, illicit levies and violence. We know that an unscrupulous despot ruled at Huaura. Returning to the Huánuco region, we may recall the case of Sebastián Núñez de Prado. For nine years this man exacted 300 baskets of coca per annum instead of the prescribed 80. And to levy the textile tribute, he imprisoned a certain number of Indians in a corral where they were forced to work without respite. As for his neighbour, García Ortiz de Espinosa, he was ordered to make restitution of 1000 pesos to his tributaries, and was even jailed for ill-treating his Indians. But malpractices of the *encomenderos* were rarely punished.

Above all, there was a qualitative change. The ideology which had justified the Inca system lay in ruins: in a society dominated by the Spanish, notions of reciprocity and redistribution had become meaningless. Or, more exactly, the Spanish system made use of fragments of the former system; reciprocity still played a part in the relations between *ayllus* and *curacas* and the latter still acted as intermediaries between the Indians and their new masters; but while reciprocity had maintained a rotation of wealth (even though fictitious or unequal) between *ayllu*, *curaca* and Inca, Spanish rule brought about a one-way transfer of goods from Indians to Spaniards, without return. Let us remember a few significant facts: at Huaura the tributaries received neither food nor tools for their work; at Huánuco, the Chupacho Indians unanimously complained that they were obliged to provide cotton for the textile tribute; at Chucuito, whereas the *curaca* still provided wool for his Indians when they wove cloth for him, the King did nothing of the kind for the thousand pieces of *ropa* he received; and the 18,000 pesos paid to His Majesty did not return in any form whatever to the Indians. The Spanish ruler had taken the

place of the Inca, he had inherited his centralizing role, but he no longer ensured redistribution of wealth for the benefit of all. In conclusion, whereas Inca tribute had functioned as a balanced and circular economic structure, Spanish tribute was chiefly remarkable for its unbalanced, unilateral structure.

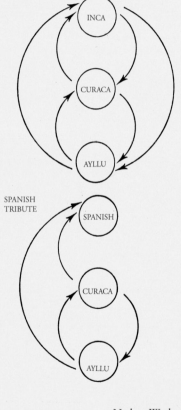

INCA TRIBUTE

SPANISH TRIBUTE

Nathan Wachtel
The Vision of the Vanquished (1971)
Translated by Ben and Siân Reynolds
1977

Martín Llapa's Complaint Against Don Francisco Fernández

This document of 1750 is one of the numerous complaints lodged with the Spanish tribunals by the Andean natives to protest abuses by the Spanish landowners.

Martín Llapa, a native Indian from the place known as Los Azogues, subject of Don Matias Tenempaguay, principal *cacique* of the Indians of the subject faction called Mageo in the said village....I declare that Don Francisco Fernández, a neighbour in the said town, without the slightest title or right to an allocation of Indians to serve in his hacienda, Tarque, and without my having been designated by my above-mentioned *cacique,* by his own authority and powerful hand, inopportunely seized me in my house and, with the worst disgrace, harshness and tyranny, took me to his aforesaid hacienda, telling me that he had the authority to force me to serve him for as many years as he wished, and he did so, and promptly put me in charge of a flock of sheep without giving me a chance to put my poor house in order or the little sowed crops I had which were now ripe, or to gather my fruits, and all this was lost because of him, and it is now my due to recuperate this without the slightest difficulty, and being an ignorant and timid Indian, and believing that my *cacique* had designated me for service, I obeyed him and humbled myself to serve him for a year and two months, unjustly, because I had not been so designated at all, so that he had committed an offence against my *cacique* by usurping his right, and an offence against me by making me work without the slightest reward, because he did not even give me the third of a full

SESTA CALLE
CORO·TASQVE

The burden of Spanish labor: An Inca girl is forced to spin, herd, and carry wood at the same time.

year's tribute, a sum which I owe the collector, and which necessarily has to be paid by him for having caused the debt while I was working for him, and even less did he give me monthly wages, because the first month he only gave me two and a half *fanegas* of barley, and through the whole year and two months there was no other reward than what I have just declared, and although I asked him for assistance he refused harshly. What's more, he did not even give me the cape that was mine by right, saying that the allocated Indian servant could ask for neither wages nor clothing, and seeing that the situation was one of resistance and destitution, I survived this whole period by borrowing wages from several Indians, not without difficulty, and I am now indebted to them as well, because my house was more than a day's walk away, which did not make my survival any easier; on top of all this there were greater wrongs, such as when Don Francisco had entrusted me with the flock, he warned his major-domo to send me out every day to labour, sow and weed and do the other usual tasks of the hacienda, without giving me the slightest salary, whereas this kind of work ought to have a different wage, and if by chance I refused I was immediately punished with beatings and floggings, and because of this the whole year went by with me serving in the fields, and I left my poor wife in charge of the flock, though she also had to carry out her personal chores, as was proper, and she was also set to the task of spinning wool and cotton fibres by Doña Petrona Abad, legitimate wife of the afore-mentioned Don Francisco Fernández, saying that as mistress of the house she had the power and authority to make her spin everything she gave her, and if she did not hand in the finished work within eight days, the major-domo was ordered to collect the work, and, if it was unfinished, to punish her, an order which the aforesaid major-domo carried out with the greatest cruelty, beating and flogging her, and seeing how we were so exhausted by this kind of work and such inhuman treatment, which is not meted out anywhere else in the world to wretched Indians, I withdrew from the said hacienda and rushed to my aforementioned *cacique* to tell him of the tasks which my wife and I had suffered because of him.... And I learned that the said Don Francisco, in revenge for my fleeing his hacienda, is lodging unjust accusations about loss of sheep, in order to make me a slave to his service, because even if it were true that a few sheep were missing, I am under no obligation to pay him the slightest *real* if my work and that of my wife has not first been paid for, considering the fact that I spent more time labouring in the fields, and when Indians guard livestock they must not be occupied with anything else if they are to be held responsible for eventual losses, and although the aforesaid flock was entrusted to my wife, she, having to do spinning chores as well, could not pasture them freely but rather exposed to danger, since she did not even have a son to help her, and in order to make me pay he has taken my poor elderly mother, and I am assured he is keeping her prisoner in the said hacienda, without informing any judge....

Translated from an original text in the Quito National Historical Archives, Indigenous Section

The colonial authorities built the town of Guanuco using a native workforce.

In Search of the Ancient Incas

One of the earliest archaeological studies of the Andes was conducted in the second half of the 19th century by American archaeologist Ephraim George Squier. Trained as a surveyor, Squier carried out detailed investigations of the ancient ruins and produced accurate plans and measurements. In this extract from his travelogue he follows an ancient Inca roadway.

Portrait of Squier.

Between Cuzco and the sweet valley of Yucay, there are numerous traces of an ancient road, some sections of which are perfect. These sections coincide in character with the long reaches in the direction of Quito. They consist of a pathway from ten to twelve feet wide, raised slightly in the centre, paved with stones, and the edges defined by lines of larger stones sunk firmly in the ground. Where this road descends from the elevated *puna*—a sheer descent of almost four thousand feet into the valley of Yucay—it zigzags on a narrow shelf cut in the face of the declivity, and supported here and there, where foothold could not otherwise be obtained, by high retaining-walls of cut stone, looking as perfect and firm as when first built centuries ago.

High mountain-ranges and broad and frigid deserts, swept by fierce, cold winds, are not the sole obstacles to intercommunication in the Altos of Peru, and among those snow-crowned monarchs of the Andes and Cordilleras. There are deep valleys, gorges, and ravines among these mountains, or cut deep in the plains that alternate with them, in which flow swelling rivers or rapid torrents, fed by the melting snows in the dry season, and swollen by the rains in the wet season. They are often unfordable; but still they must somehow be passed by the traveller. A few bridges of stone were constructed by the Spaniards, some after the Conquest; but, as a rule, the rivers and mountain torrents are passed to-day by the aid of devices the same as were resorted to by the Incas, and at points which they selected. Had the principle of the arch been well understood by the ancient inhabitants, who have left some of the finest stone-cutting and masonry to be found in the world, there is no doubt the interior of Peru would have abounded in bridges rivalling those of Rome in extent and beauty. As it was, occupying a country destitute of timber, they resorted to suspension bridges, no doubt precisely like those now constructed by their descendants and successors—bridges formed of cables of braided withes, stretched from bank to bank, and called *puentes de mimbres* (bridges of withes). Where the banks are high, or where the streams are compressed between steep or precipitous rocks, these cables are anchored to piers of stone. In other places they are approached by inclined causeways, raised to give them the necessary elevation above the water. Three or four cables form the floor and the principal support of the bridge, over which small sticks, sometimes only sections of cane or bamboo, are laid transversely, and fastened to the cables by vines, cords, or thongs of raw hide. Two smaller cables are sometimes stretched on each side, as a guard or hand-rail. Over these frail and swaying structures pass men and animals, the latter frequently with their loads on their backs....

The Apurimac is one of the head-waters of the Amazon, a large and rapid stream, flowing in a deep valley, or, rather, gigantic ravine, shut in by high and precipitous mountains. Throughout its length it is crossed at only a single point, between two enormous cliffs, which rise dizzily on both sides, and from the summits of which the traveller looks down into a dark gulf. At the bottom gleams a white line of water, whence struggles up a dull but heavy roar, giving to the river its name, *Apu-rimac*, signifying, in the

The bridge over the Apurimac River, an engraving from Squier's book.

Quichua tongue, "the great speaker." From above, the bridge, looking like a mere thread, is reached by a path which on one side traces a thin, white line on the face of the mountain, and down which the boldest traveller may hesitate to venture.... It is usual for the traveller to time his day's journey so as to reach this bridge in the morning, before the strong wind sets in; for, during the greater part of the day, it sweeps up the cañon of the Apurimac with great force, and then the bridge sways like a gigantic hammock, and crossing is next to impossible.

Ephraim George Squier,
Peru: Incidents of Travel and Exploration in the Land of the Incas,
1877

The Discovery of Machu Picchu

A professional archaeologist, Hiram Bingham (1875–1956) was passionately interested in all the curiosities of South America. Familiar with the texts of the early chroniclers, Bingham drew on these narratives to reach the "lost city," thus giving historical reality to a site that, until then, had lived only in legend.

We passed an ill-kept, grass-thatched hut, turned off the road through a tiny clearing, and made our camp at the edge of the river on a sandy beach. Opposite us, beyond the huge granite boulders which interfered with the progress of the surging stream, the steep mountain was clothed with thick jungle. Since we were near the road yet protected from the curiosity of passers-by, it seemed to be an ideal spot for a camp. Our actions, however, aroused the suspicions of the owner of the hut, Melchor Arteaga, who leased the lands of Mandor Pampa. He was anxious to know why we did not stay at his "tavern" like other respectable travellers. Fortunately the Prefect of Cuzco, our old friend J. J. Nuñez, had given us an armed escort who spoke Quichua. Our gendarme, Sergeant Carrasco, was able to reassure the innkeeper. They had quite a long conversation. When Arteaga learned that we were interested in the architectural remains of the Incas, and were looking for the palace of the last Inca, he said there were some very good ruins in this vicinity—in fact, some excellent ones on top of the opposite mountain, called Huayna Picchu, and also on a ridge called Machu Picchu.

The morning of July 24th dawned in a cold drizzle. Arteaga shivered and seemed inclined to stay in his hut. I offered to pay him well if he would show me the ruins. He demurred and said it was too hard a climb for such a wet day. But when he found that I was willing to pay him a *sol* (a Peruvian silver dollar, 50 cents, gold), three or four times the ordinary daily wage in this vicinity, he finally agreed to go. When asked just where the ruins were, he pointed straight

The Temple of the Three Windows at Machu Picchu.

The expedition followed the gorges of the Urubamba River.

hour Arteaga left the main road and plunged down through the jungle to the bank of the river. Here there was a primitive bridge which crossed the roaring rapids at its narrowest part, where the stream was forced to flow between two great boulders. The "bridge" was made of half a dozen very slender logs, some of which were not long enough to span the distance between the boulders, but had been spliced and lashed together with vines!

Arteaga and the sergeant took off their shoes and crept gingerly across.... It was obvious that no one could live for an instant in the icy cold rapids, but would immediately be dashed to pieces against the rocks. I frankly confess that I got down on my hands and knees and crawled across, 6 inches at a time. Even after we reached the other side I could not help wondering what would happen to the bridge if a particularly heavy shower should fall in the valley above. A light rain had fallen during the night and the river had risen so that the bridge was already threatened by the foaming rapids. It would not take much more to wash it away entirely. If this should happen during the day it might be very awkward. As a matter of fact, it did happen a few days later and when the next visitors attempted to cross the river at this point they found only one slender log remaining.

Leaving the stream, we now struggled up the bank through dense jungle, and in a few minutes reached the bottom of a very precipitous slope. For an hour and twenty minutes we had a hard climb. A good part of the distance we went on all fours, sometimes holding on by our fingernails. Here and there, a primitive ladder made from the roughly notched trunk of a small tree was placed in such a way as to help one over what might

to the top of the mountain. No one supposed that they would be particularly interesting. And no one cared to go with me. Our naturalist said there were "more butterflies near the river!" and he was reasonably certain he could collect some new varieties. Our surgeon said he had to wash his clothes and mend them. Anyhow it was my job to investigate all reports of ruins and try to find the Inca capital.

So, accompanied only by Sergeant Carrasco, I left camp at ten o'clock. Arteaga took us some distance upstream. On the road we passed a snake which had only just been killed. He said the region was the favourite haunt of "vipers"....

After a walk of three quarters of an

H ouses and surrounding walls of Machu Picchu (above and opposite).

otherwise have proved to be an impassable cliff. In another place the slope was covered with slippery grass where it was hard to find either handholds or footholds. Arteaga groaned and said that there were lots of snakes here. Sergeant Carrasco said nothing but was glad he had good military shoes....

Shortly after noon, just as we were completely exhausted, we reached a little grass-covered hut 2000 feet above the river where several good-natured Indians, pleasantly surprised at our unexpected arrival, welcomed us with dripping gourds full of cool, delicious water. Then they set before us a few cooked sweet potatoes. It seems that two Indian farmers, Richarte and Alvarez, had recently chosen this eagles' nest for their home. They said they had found plenty of terraces here on which to grow their crops. Laughingly they admitted they enjoyed being free from undesirable visitors, officials looking for army "volunteers" or collecting taxes.

Richarte told us that they had been living here for years. It seems probable that, owing to its inaccessibility, the canyon has been unoccupied for several centuries, but with the completion of the new government road, settlers began once more to occupy this region....

They said there were two paths to the

F irst topographic survey of the site of Machu Picchu, made by Bingham in 1912.

outside world. Of one we had already had a taste; the other was "even more difficult," a perilous path down the face of a rocky precipice on the other side of the ridge. It was their only means of egress in the wet season when the primitive bridge over which we had come could not be maintained. I was not surprised to learn that they went away from home "only about once a month."

Through Sergeant Carrasco I learned that the ruins were "a little further along." In this country one never can tell whether such a report is worthy of credence. "He may have been lying" is a good footnote to affix to all hearsay evidence. Accordingly, I was not unduly excited, nor in a great hurry to move. The heat was still great, the water from the Indians' spring was cool and delicious, and the rustic wooden bench, hospitably covered immediately after my arrival with a soft woollen *poncho*, most comfortable. Furthermore, the view was simply enchanting. Tremendous green precipices fell away to the white rapids of the Urubamba below. Immediately in front, on the north side of the valley, was a great granite cliff rising 2000 feet sheer. To the left was the solitary peak of Huayna Picchu, surrounded by seemingly inaccessible precipices. On all sides were rocky cliffs. Beyond them cloud-capped, snow-covered mountains rose thousands of feet above us.

We continued to enjoy the wonderful view of the canyon, but all the ruins we could see from our cool shelter were a few terraces.

Without the slightest expectation of finding anything more interesting than the ruins of two or three stone houses such as we had encountered at various places on the road between Ollantaytambo and Torontoy, I finally left the cool shade of the pleasant little hut and climbed further up the ridge and round a slight promontory. Melchor Arteaga had "been there once before," so he decided to rest and gossip with Richarte and Alvarez. They sent a small boy with me as a "guide." The sergeant was in duty bound to follow, but I think he may have been a little curious to see what there was to see.

Hardly had we left the hut and rounded the promontory than we were confronted with an unexpected sight, a great flight of beautifully constructed stone-faced terraces, perhaps a hundred of them, each hundreds of feet long and 10 feet high. They had been recently rescued from the jungle by the Indians. A veritable forest of large trees which had been growing on them for centuries had been chopped down and partly burned to make a clearing for agricultural purposes. The task was too great for the two Indians so the tree trunks had been allowed to lie as they fell and only the smaller branches removed. But the ancient soil, carefully put in place by the Incas, was still capable of producing rich crops of maize and potatoes.

However, there was nothing to be excited about. Similar flights of well-made terraces are to be seen in the upper Urubamba Valley at Pisac and Ollantaytambo, as well as opposite Torontoy. So we patiently followed the little guide along one of the widest terraces, where there had once been a small conduit, and made our way into an untouched forest beyond. Suddenly I found myself confronted with the walls of ruined houses built of the finest quality of Inca stone work. It was hard to see them for they were partly covered with trees and moss, the growth of centuries, but in the dense shadow, hiding in bamboo thickets and tangled vines, appeared here and there walls of white granite ashlars carefully cut and exquisitely fitted together. We scrambled along through the dense undergrowth, climbing over terrace walls and in bamboo thickets, where our guide found it easier going than I did. Suddenly, without any warning, under a huge overhanging ledge the boy showed me a cave beautifully lined with the finest cut stone. It had evidently been a royal mausoleum.

On top of this particular ledge was a semicircular building whose outer wall, gently sloping and slightly curved, bore a striking resemblance to the famous temple of the Sun in Cuzco. This might also be a temple of the sun. It followed the natural curvature of the rock and was keyed to it by one of the finest examples of masonry I had ever seen. Furthermore it was tied into another beautiful wall, made of very carefully matched ashlars of pure white granite, especially selected for its fine grain. Clearly, it was the work of a master artist. The interior surface of the wall was broken by niches and square stone-pegs. The exterior surface was perfectly simple and unadorned. The lower courses, of particularly large ashlars, gave it a look of solidity. The upper courses, diminishing in size towards the top, lent grace and delicacy to the structure. The flowing lines, the symmetrical arrangement of the

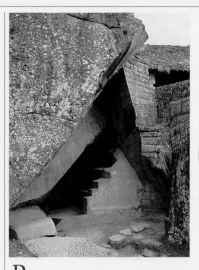

Royal tomb behind the temple of the sun.

ashlars, and the gradual gradation of the courses, combined to produce a wonderful effect, softer and more pleasing than that of the marble temples of the Old World. Owing to the absence of mortar, there were no ugly spaces between the rocks. They might have grown together. On account of the beauty of the white granite this structure surpassed in attractiveness the best Inca walls in Cuzco, which had caused visitors to marvel for four centuries. It seemed like an unbelievable dream. Dimly, I began to realize that this wall and its adjoining semicircular temple over the cave were as fine as the finest stonework in the world.

It fairly took my breath away. What could this place be? Why had no one given us any idea of it? Even Melchor Arteaga was only moderately interested and had no appreciation of the importance of the ruins which Richarte and Alvarez had adopted for their little farm. Perhaps after all this was an isolated small place which had escaped notice because it was inaccessible.

Then the little boy urged us to climb up a steep hill over what seemed to be a flight of stone steps. Surprise followed surprise in bewildering succession. We came to a great stairway of large granite blocks. Then we walked along a path to a clearing where the Indians had planted a small vegetable garden. Suddenly we found ourselves standing in front of the ruins of two of the finest and most interesting structures in ancient America. Made of beautiful white granite, the walls contained blocks of Cyclopean size, higher than a man. The sight had me spellbound.

Each building had only three walls and was entirely open on one side. The principal temple had walls 12 feet high which were lined with exquisitely made niches, five high up at each end, and seven on the back. There were seven courses of ashlars in the end walls. Under the seven rear niches was a rectangular block 14 feet long, possibly a sacrificial altar, but more probably a throne for the mummies of departed Incas, brought out to be worshipped. The building did not look as though it had ever had a roof. The top course of beautifully smooth ashlars was left uncovered so that the sun could be welcomed here by priests and mummies. I could scarcely believe my senses as I examined the larger blocks in the lower course and estimated that they must weigh from ten to fifteen tons each. Would anyone believe what I had found? Fortunately, in this land where accuracy in reporting what one has seen is not a prevailing characteristic of travellers, I had a good camera and the sun was shining.

The principal temple faces the south where there is a small plaza or courtyard. On the east side of the plaza was another amazing structure, the ruins of a temple containing three great windows looking out over the canyon to the rising sun. Like its neighbour, it is unique among Inca ruins. Nothing just like them in design and execution has ever been found. Its three conspicuously large windows, obviously too large to serve any useful purpose, were most beautifully made with the greatest care and solidity. This was clearly a ceremonial edifice of peculiar significance. Nowhere else in Peru, so far as I know, is there a similar structure conspicuous for being "a masonry wall with three windows." It will be remembered that Salcamayhua, the Peruvian who wrote an account of the antiquities of Peru in 1620, said that the first Inca, Manco the Great, ordered "works to be executed at the place of his birth, consisting of a masonry wall with three windows." Was that what I had found? If it was, then this was not the capital of the last Inca, but the birthplace of the first. It did not occur to me that it might be both. To be sure the region was one which could fit in with the requirements of Tampu-tocco, the place of refuge of the civilized folk who fled from the southern barbarian tribes after the battle of La Raya and brought with them the body of their king Pachacuti VI who was slain by an arrow. He might have been buried in the stone-lined cave under the semi-circular temple.

Hiram Bingham
Lost City of the Incas
1948

The Mysteries of Nazca

Comprising the peoples of three valleys—those of Nazca, Ica, and Pisco—on the southern coast of Peru, the Nazca culture, which reached its zenith between 350 BC and AD 650, has a primary place in the history of pre-Inca peoples. Although also known for its ceramics and textiles, Nazca is most famous for its geoglyphs—immense drawings traced on the plains that still raise all kinds of questions for anthropologists.

From Lima the Pan American Highway winds south along the Peruvian coast through a succession of river valleys until it reaches the sleepy town of Nazca.... For the residents it is a farming center, one that was old before the Spanish arrived and even before the Incas came to power. Its broad valley is green with cotton, corn, and a myriad of other crops. All around rise the foothills that parade up to the mighty Andes.

It is not produce, however, that has put Nazca on the world map. To the northwest of town a triangular stretch of somewhat level desert up to 15 km wide—the pampa—contains an astounding assortment of animal figures, lines, avenues, and trapezoids etched into the timeless surface....

The geoglyphs, as they're called, are of two sorts. First are the "animals"— fantastic drawings of a monkey, spider, fox, and more—concentrated in a small section in the northeastern part of the pampa.... From the ground the forms are practically impossible to see since they are up to scores of meters in extent. Only from the air can these wonders be viewed in their entirety.... From many of the low hills on and around the pampa emanate numerous rays (narrow straight lines), avenues (broad lines), and trapezoids (avenues that broaden out and end squared off). So different are these from the animals that most Nazca researchers feel they are not from the same cultural epoch. Rays are also found quite far north and south, but nowhere in such profusion as at Nazca.

The animals may have had a religious or sociological meaning. Maria Reiche, who has studied the figures for almost

Ceramic drum found at Nazca.

Geoglyph known as "the Whale" on the plains of Nazca.

four decades, thinks that at least some of them represent constellations (the Spider being Orion, for example), but there are no convincing demonstrations of such relationships. It has been suggested that the figures were designed to be walked as a spiritual exercise or were associated with particular families. The puzzling fact that the figures can be seen whole only from the air has also fueled speculations that the natives were balloonists or that the figures were made by ancient astronauts! Yet there is no evidence their makers intended them to be seen at all—maybe they were to be experienced in some other way.

The manner in which the animals were conceived and made is not very problematic. Andean and coastal cultures have a long tradition of exquisite textile design, and scaling up a figure should have been straightforward. The patterns were made on the desert by simply removing rocks from an area and stacking them up to form a border. Walking or sweeping the resulting figures disturbs a thin brown coating of material called desert varnish. This action exposes the creamy pink soil underneath....

From an astronomical point of view the rays are much more promising. It has been suggested that those not aligned with horizon features mark the directions of important sunrises and sunsets (of the solstices, for example). According to Reiche, the trapezoids indicate the extremes of moonrise and set. On the other hand, equally reasonable explanations of the features

Geoglyph at Nazca called "the Monkey."

relate them to native families or to water flow across the pampa—a critical matter in a desert environment....

[Anthropologist Persis B.] Clarkson has been working on and off the pampa for the past three years studying the local pottery in particular and its association with the lines. Most of what has been found is pottery for carrying water, dating from the Late Intermediate period (AD 1000–1400). As Clarkson walks the lines she notes which ones cross over others, to derive a sequence for their construction.

Unfortunately, in the area of the animals Reiche has swept all the figures, thus obliterating any trace of the line chronology. A hint that the animals date back to the Nazca period (roughly 600 BC–AD 500) is found in the similarity of the animals to designs on the pottery of that culture. When her work is complete, Clarkson hopes to be able to say when the geoglyphs were made and the cultural basis for their creation....

The astronomy of the native Peruvians is quite different from the Middle Eastern-European astronomy of the Northern Hemisphere.... Most important...is the dominance of the Milky Way as seen from the south of the equator. So strongly does it figure in Peruvian astronomy that the cardinal directions are northeast, southeast, southwest, and northwest—the extremes of the Milky Way's intersection with the horizon.... In addition to the usual point-to-point constellations picked out by bright stars, there are constellations defined by dark areas of the celestial river that is our galaxy. The Sun was important for calendrical purposes as was the heliacal rising and settings of

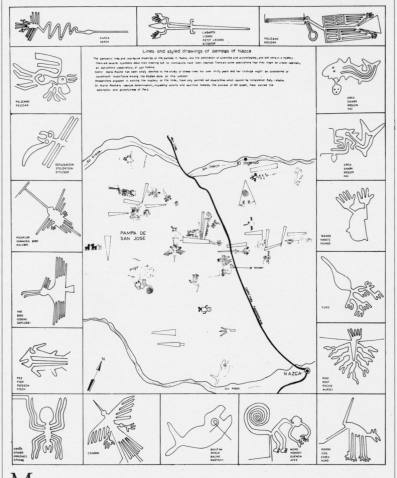

M ap and drawings of the Nazca geoglyphs.

certain constellations (especially the Pleiades, called the Storehouse). These are all facts that must be woven into any study of possible astronomical alignments of the Nazca lines....

But whatever the original purpose or purposes of the lines, they remain one of the great wonders of the Andean world and an awe-inspiring sight for anyone fortunate enough to see them.

William E. Shawcross,
"Mystery on the Desert—
The Nazca Lines,"
Sky & Telescope, September 1984

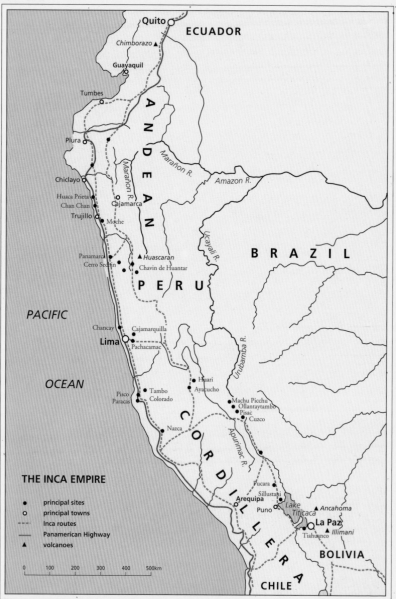

THE INCA EMPIRE

- • principal sites
- ○ principal towns
- - - - Inca routes
- —— Panamerican Highway
- ▲ volcanoes

0   100   200   300   400   500km

Further Reading

Andrien, Kenneth J., and Rolena Adorno, eds., *Transatlantic Encounters: Europeans and Andeans in the 16th Century,* University of California Press, Berkeley, 1991

Bingham, Hiram, *Lost City of the Incas: The Story of Machu Picchu and Its Builders,* reprint of 1948 edition, Greenwood, New York, 1981

Cameron, Ian, *Kingdom of the Sun God: A History of the Andes and Their People,* Facts on File, New York, 1990

Cieza de León, Pedro, *Chronicle of Peru,* trans. Clements R. Markham, Hakluyt Society, London, 1864

Elliott, J. H., *The Spanish World,* Harry N. Abrams, New York, 1991

Garcilaso de la Vega, *Royal Commentaries of the Incas and General History of Peru,* reprint of 1869 edition, University of Texas Press, Austin, 1987

Hemming, John, *The Conquest of the Incas,* Harcourt Brace Jovanovich, New York, 1983

Humboldt, Alexander von, *Personal Narrative of Travels to the Equinoctial Regions of the New Continent, 1797–1804,* Longman and Hurst, London, 1814

Keatinge, Richard W., ed., *Peruvian Prehistory,* Cambridge University Press, Cambridge, England, 1988

Kendall, Ann, *Everyday Life of the Incas,* Batsford, London, 1989

McNeill, William H., *Plagues and Peoples,* Penguin, London, 1976

Métraux, Alfred, *The History of the Incas,* Schocken Books, New York, 1970

Molina, Cristobal de, *The Fables and Rites of the Incas,* trans. Clements R. Markham, Hakluyt Society, London, 1873

Morris, Craig, and Donald E. Thompson, *Huanuco Pampa: An Inca City and Its Hinterland,* Thames and Hudson, London and New York, 1985

Moseley, Michael E., *The Incas and Their Ancestors: The Archaeology of Peru,* Thames and Hudson, London and New York, 1992

Murra, John, *The Economic Organization of the Inca State,* Jai Press, Greenwich, Connecticut, 1980

Nash, Nathaniel C., "Archaeologist Wants to Reconquer Shrine for Incas," *The New York Times,* 31 August 1993

Oxford Analytica, *Latin America in Perspective,* Houghton Mifflin, Boston, 1991

Pizarro, Pedro, *Relation of the Discovery and Conquest of the Kingdoms of Peru,* Kraus Books, Millwood, New York, 1921

Prescott, William H., *History of the Conquest of Peru,* Harper and Brothers, New York, 1847

Rowe, John H., "Inca Culture at the Time of the Spanish Conquest," *Handbook of South American Indians,* ed. John Steward, Government Printing Office, Washington, D.C., 1946–59

Shawcross, William E., "Mystery on the Desert—The Nazca Lines," *Sky & Telescope,* September 1984

Squier, Ephraim George, *Peru: Incidents of Travel and Exploration in the Land of the Incas,* Peabody Museum, Harvard University, Boston, 1877

Wachtel, Nathan, *The Vision of the Vanquished,* Barnes and Noble, New York, 1977

Xeres, Francisco de, *Reports on the Discovery of Peru,* trans. Clements R. Markham, Hakluyt Society, London, 1872

List of Illustrations

Key: a=above; *b*=below; *c*=center; *l*=left; *r*=right

Abbreviations:
BMNHN=Bibliothèque du Muséum National d'Histoire Naturelle, Paris; BNM=Biblioteca Nacional, Madrid; BNP= Bibliothèque Nationale, Paris; MNM=Musée du Nouveau Monde, La Rochelle, France

Front cover Detail of a gold Chimú headband *Spine* Jama-Coaque. Chancay sculpture. Tony Morrison *Back cover* Woolen artifact. Musée de l'Homme, Paris *1–9* Bruno Mallart. Drawings after the photographs in Hiram Bingham's logbook *12* Panoramic wallpaper

with Inca motifs. Manufactured by Dufour et Leroy, 1826. MNM *13* Dupetit-Thouars. A 16th-century ship. Engraving after Brueghel. BMNHN *14* Jost Amman. Native Peruvians. Engraving, 1577. BNM *15* Map of Peru from George Le Testu, *Cosmographie Universelle.*

Bibliothèque du Ministère de la Défense, Paris *16* Felipe Guamán Poma de Ayala. Pizarro and his comrades aboard their ship. Drawing, late 16th century *16–7* An Inca raft. Illustration from George Juan and Antonio de Ulloa, *Voyage Historique de l'Amérique Méridionale,* 1752.

Institut des Hautes Etudes d'Amérique Latine, Paris

17 Textile of the Paracas culture. Private collection

18al Sword of Buabdil. Museo del Ejército

18ar Vasquez Diaz Trujillo. Portrait of Pizarro. Painting. Instituto de Cultura Hispanica, Madrid

18b Lancer and arquebusier. Colored engraving, 16th century. Historical and Military Archives of the Austrian Dynasty, Madrid

19 Members of the Inca's army. Colored engraving, 1572. BNP

20–1 Pizarro encouraging his companions to undertake the conquest of Peru. Engraving after a painting by Lizcano, 1882

21 Member of the Koto tribe with decorated earlobe. Photograph

22–3 Inca fortress of Sacsahuaman, above Cuzco. Photograph

23a and b Inca emperors Pachacuti (above) and Huascar (below). Archivo General de Indias, Seville

24–5 Portraits of Inca sovereigns. Oil on cotton, 17th century. Musée de l'Homme, Paris

26–7 Manco Capac and Queen Mama Huaco greeting their subjects. Colored Italian engraving, c. 1820

27 Ceramic sculptures of the Mochica culture. Museo Nacional de Antropologia y Arqueologia, Lima

28–9 Pizarro asking Charles V for the governorship of Peru. Engraving

29 Portrait of Huascar. Oil on cotton, 17th century. Musée de l'Homme, Paris

30 Alonzo in Tumbes. Watercolor from Jean-François Marmontel, *Les Incas,* 1777. MNM

31 The port of Callao. Watercolor from *Mapas de las Costas de Nueva España.* BNM

32–3a Walls of the Inca fortress Sacsahuaman. Photograph

32–3b Pizarro conquering Peru. Engraving from Théodore de Bry, *Historia Americae,* 1602

34 The clemency of Mayta Capac. Colored Italian engraving, c. 1820

35l Felipe Guamán Poma de Ayala. Sacrifice of an *urcu.* Drawing, late 16th century

35r Costume of an *aclla,* a virgin of the sun. Colored engraving, 18th century. Bibliothèque des Arts Décoratifs, Paris

36–7 "The Sin of Cora the Priestess." Illustration from Jean-François Marmontel, *Les Incas,* 1777. MNM

38–9 "The Punishment." *Ibid.*

40 The manufacture of Peruvian textiles. Colored drawing from Martínez Compañon, *Libro Trujillo del Perú,* 17th century. Biblioteca del Palacio Real, Madrid

41a and b Textiles of the Paracas culture. Private collection

41r Textile ornament made of braided wool. Musée de l'Homme, Paris

42 Types of Inca bridges. Colored engraving from George Juan and Antonio de Ulloa, *Voyage Historique de l'Amérique Méridionale,* 1752. Institut des Hautes Etudes d'Amérique Latine, Paris

42–3 Rope bridge near Penipé. Colored engraving from Alexander von Humboldt, *Vue des Cordillères et des Monuments des Peuples de l'Amérique,* 1810. BMNHN

43 Peruvian monument of Ingapirca. *Ibid.*

44 Costumes of the Inca and his wife. Colored drawing, 18th century. Bibliothèque des Arts Décoratifs, Paris

45a Engravings from Castelnau, *Expédition dans les Parties Centrales de l'Amérique du Sud,* 1852. BMNHN

45b The temple of the sun. Colored engraving from George Juan and Antonio de Ulloa, *Voyage Historique de l'Amérique Méridionale,* 1752. Institut des Hautes Etudes d'Amérique Latine, Paris

46 Atahualpa travels to Cajamarca to meet Pizarro. Engraving from *Histoire de l'Amérique Latine et des Antilles,* 1500–34. BNP

47a Inca emperor Atahualpa. Engraving. Private collection, Paris

47b Fabric made of feathers and plates of gold. Chancay culture. Museo de Oro del Peru, Lima

48 Inca warriors. Colored engraving from *Histoire de l'Amérique Latine et des Antilles,* 1500–34. BNP

48–9 Bergeret. Pizarro accepting the ransom of Atahualpa. Wash drawing and ink. MNM

49r Chimú knife. Museo de Arte de Lima

50–1 Atahualpa's funeral. Engraving, 19th century. Bibliothèque d'Art et d'Archéologie, Paris

51 Panoramic wallpaper with Inca motifs. Manufactured by Dufour et Leroy, 1826. MNM

52 Pizarro assassinated by conspirators. Engraving, 19th century

53 Anonymous. Portrait of Topa Amaru, the last Inca, as a prisoner. Painting, 18th century. Museo Histórico Nacional, Buenos Aires

54 Felipe Guamán Poma de Ayala. Inca farming methods. Drawing, late 16th century (colored by Laure Massin). Royal Library, Copenhagen

55 A struggle between members of two Spanish factions. Colored illustration

56–7 The Spaniards force the natives to carry their booty. Engraving, 1532

57 Titian. Portrait of Spanish prince Philip II. Painting, c. 1550. Musée du Louvre, Paris

58a Alcide-Charles-Victor Dessalines d'Orbigny. View of the village of Palca. Engraving. BMNHN

58b Native porters. Engraving from Alexander von Humboldt, *Vue des Cordillères et des Monuments des Peuples de l'Amérique,* 1810. BMNHN

59 Felipe Guamán Poma de Ayala. The *quipu,* an Inca accounting device. Drawing, late 16th century (colored by Laure Massin). BNP

60 Inca terraces at Pisac. Photograph

61 Inca agriculture. Engraving from Théodore de Bry, *Historia Americae,* 1602

62l Llamas. Engraving. Private collection

62r Woolen coca bag
63 An Inca farm. Colored drawing from Martínez Compañon, *Libro Trujillo del Perú,* 17th century. Biblioteca del Palacio Real, Madrid
64–5 Map of the Cordillera of Peru. Engraving. Bibliothèque de l'Institut de France, Paris
65 Hoppolyytorniz and Joseph Paron. Peruvian and Chilean flora. Engraving, 1802. BNP
66a Bosina shell. Engraving. Bibliothèque d'Art et d'Archéologie, Paris
66b Inca hunting scenes. Colored drawings from Martínez Compañon, *Libro Trujillo del Perú,* 17th century. Biblioteca del Palacio Real, Madrid
67 Idem
68 Inca canal at Cajamarca, Peru. Photograph
68–9 Inca marriage ceremony. Colored Italian engraving, c. 1820
70 Prospecting for gold. Colombian engraving. Museo del Oro, Bogotá
70–1 Mount Potosí. Colored engraving
72 Brother Luis Bolaños Apostal del Paraguay and an Inca headman. Museo San Roque, Buenos Aires
73 Archangel. Peruvian painting, 17th century. Private collection
74a Mummy adorned with jewels and wrapped in fabrics. Paracas culture. Museo de Oro del Peru, Lima
74c Detail of llama wool fabric used to wrap mummies. Paracas culture. Museo de Arte de Lima
74b Diadem of plumes on a skull. Nazca culture. Museo de Oro del Peru, Lima

75 Pre-Inca cemetery. Photograph
76a Mummy wrapped in fabric. Paracas culture. Museo Nacional de Antropologia y Arqueologia, Lima
76–7 Burial of kings in Peru. Engraving, 16th century. BNP
77 Alcide-Charles-Victor Dessalines d'Orbigny. Engraving of Inca ceramics. BMMNH
78 Spanish clerics. Colored drawings from Martínez Compañon, *Libro Trujillo del Perú,* 17th century. Biblioteca del Palacio Real, Madrid
78–9 The city of Cuzco. Colored Dutch engraving, 16th century
79 Doll of the Chancay culture, Peru
80–1 A festival at Lima. Print, 19th century. BNP
81 Peruvian ecclesiastical costumes. Print, 1937. BNP
82 Church of Santo Domingo in Cuzco. Photograph
83a Felipe Guamán Poma de Ayala. The Inca god Viracocha. Drawing, late 16th century. BNP
83b Inca terra-cotta figurine
84 Costume of an Inca priest from a French ballet. Watercolor. MNM
85l A priest and a native. Colored drawing from Martínez Compañon, *Libro Trujillo del Perú,* 17th century. Biblioteca del Palacio Real, Madrid
85r Quena player
86 The Festival of the Dead at Cuzco. Engraving
86–7 Priest and women of Lima. Colored engraving, c. 1848. Bibliothèque des Arts Décoratifs, Paris
88 Funerary doll of the Chancay culture

88–9 Painted textile of the Nazca culture. The Cleveland Museum of Art
89 Textile mask of the Chancay culture
90 The Dance of Lions festival. Colored drawing from Martínez Compañon, *Libro Trujillo del Perú,* 17th century. Biblioteca del Palacio Real, Madrid
90–1 Gathering herbs. Colored engraving from Alexander von Humboldt, *Vue des Cordillères et des Monuments des Peuples de l'Amérique,* 1810. BMNHN
91 Trepanned skull. Museo Nacional de Antropologia y Arqueologia, Lima
92 Inca emperor. Oil on canvas, 17th century
93 Linati-El Cura manuscript of Miguel Hidalgo Castilla. Museo de América, Madrid
94al Tapestry fragment of the Paracas culture
94ar Wooden kero of the Inca culture. Museo Archeológico, La Paz
94b Alcide-Charles-Victor Dessalines d'Orbigny. Engravings of pre-Inca vessels. BMNHN
95 Painted wooden chest from the early 16th century. Casa de Murillo, La Paz
96al E. Vidal. A woman with a llama, from a series of South American costumes. Watercolor, c. 1820
96ar Ramon Salas. Water-carrier. Watercolor, 19th century. Casa de Cultura, Quito
96b Servant of Lima. Illustration from Dupetit-Thouars, *Voyage Autour du Monde,* 1836–9. BMNHN

97 Religious education. Colored illustration from Martínez Compañon, *Libro Trujillo del Perú,* 17th century. Biblioteca del Palacio Real, Madrid
98–103 The peoples and produce of Peru. Painting, c. 1700
104–5 Primeros Mulatos de Esmerridas. Museo de América, Madrid
105 A bullfight. Illustration from Martínez Compañon, *Libro Trujillo del Perú,* 17th century. Private collection
106 Ramon Salas. Procession and religious festival. Watercolor, 19th century. Casa de Cultura, Quito
107 Officer of the Peruvian militia. Colored engraving from Dupetit-Thouars, *Voyage Autour du Monde,* 1836–9. BMNHN
108–9 Jesus-Maria Zamora. Bolívar and Santander in the country of the Llanos. Painting
109 Portrait of Simon Bolívar. Instituto de Cooperación, Madrid
110 Portrait of José de San Martín. Engraving
110–1 Jura de la Independencia del Perú. Painting. Museo Nacional de Historia, Lima
112 Machu Picchu. Photograph
113 View of the Cordillera. Colored engraving from Alexander von Humboldt, *Vue des Cordillères et des Monuments des Peuples de l'Amérique,* 1810. BMNHN
114 Hiram Bingham. Bridge over the rapids of the Urubamba River. Photograph from Bingham, *Report of the Peruvian Expedition,* 1912. BNP

115 Discovery of Inca ruins. *Ibid.*

116–7 Fortress of Ollantaytambo, near Cuzco, at the entrance of the sacred valley of the Incas. Photograph

117 Hiram Bingham. White rock over a spring. Photograph from Bingham, *Report of the Peruvian Expedition,* 1912. BNP

118–9 The city of Machu Picchu. Photograph

120–1 Serge Hochain. Artist's reconstruction of Machu Picchu

122–3 Hiram Bingham. View of Machu Picchu and the canyon of the Urubamba River. Photograph from Bingham, *Report of the Peruvian Expedition,* 1912. BNP

123 The valley of the Urubamba River as it looks today. Photograph

124l Hiram Bingham. The city gate of Machu Picchu. Photograph from Bingham, *Report of the Peruvian Expedition,* 1912. BNP

124r Doors of Inca houses. Drawings

125 *Intihuatana* at Machu Picchu. Photograph

126 Peruvian on the road near Pisac. Photograph

126–7 Peruvian fisherman on a lake. Photograph

127 Woman in a field. Photograph

128 Detail of a floor covering of the Cuzco School, mid-18th century. Museo de Arte Colonial, Cuzco

129 Felipe Guamán Poma de Ayala. A procession of drummers. Drawing, late 16th century

130 Pizarro's house at Cuzco. Engraving from Castelnau, *Expédition dans les Parties Centrales de l'Amérique du Sud,* 1852. BMNHN

131 Felipe Guamán Poma de Ayala. The Inca Atahualpa. Drawing, late 16th century

132 Pizarro taking Cuzco, 15 November 1533. Engraving from *Histoire de l'Amérique Latine et des Antilles,* 1500–34. BNP

134 Topa Yopanqui. Engraving. Archivo General de Indias, Seville

136 Frontispiece from *Historia General de los Hechos de los Castellanos.* Archivo General de Indias, Seville

137 Pizarro captures Atahualpa and defeats his army near Cajamarca. Engraving. BNM

138 Felipe Guamán Poma de Ayala. Pizarro is welcomed to Cuzco. Drawing, late 16th century

140 Jean Picart. Inca hair-cutting ceremony. Engraving, 1723. Bibliothèque des Arts Décoratifs, Paris

142 A *quipu.* Musée de l'Homme, Paris

144 Portrait of Manco Capac. Engraving. Archivo General de Indias, Seville

145 Felipe Guamán Poma de Ayala. Evangelists teaching. Drawing, late 16th century

147 Sacks of coca leaves. Photograph

148 Peruvian costumes. Illustration from Martínez Compañon, *Libro Trujillo del Perú,* 17th century. Biblioteca del Palacio Real, Madrid

149 Felipe Guamán Poma de Ayala. An Inca religious ritual. Drawing, late 16th century

150a Funerary mask

150b Silver llama

151 Jean Picart. The Inca consecrating his vase of *chicha* to the sun. Engraving, 1723. Bibliothèque des Arts Décoratifs, Paris

153 Jean Picart. Sacrifice of a black llama during a festival of the sun. Engraving, 1723. Bibliothèque des Arts Décoratifs, Paris

154 Felipe Guamán Poma de Ayala. The Christian god holding symbols of heavenly beings worshiped by the Incas. Drawing, late 16th century

155 Reconstruction of a temple of the sun. Bibliothèque des Arts Décoratifs, Paris

157 Coricancha, Inca temple of the sun, surmounted by the Spanish church of Santo Domingo. Photograph

158 Natives dancing. Engraving, c. 1848. Bibliothèque des Arts Décoratifs, Paris

159 Felipe Guamán Poma de Ayala. Inca burial rites. Drawing, late 16th century

161l and r Depictions of people of racially mixed descent. Paintings, 18th century. Museo de América, Madrid

163 Felipe Guamán Poma de Ayala. Harvesting maize. Drawing, late 16th century

164 Juan de la Cruz. Native Peruvian woman. Engraving. Bibliothèque des Arts Décoratifs, Paris

165 Felipe Guamán Poma de Ayala. Laborers building walls. Drawing, late 16th century

166 Colonial rule. Illustration from Martínez Compañon,

Libro Trujillo del Perú, 17th century. Biblioteca del Palacio Real, Madrid

168a Alcide-Charles-Victor Dessalines d'Orbigny. Chulumani. Engraving, early 19th century. BMNHN

168b Chorillos man dressed for a festival. Engraving from Dupetit-Thouars, *Voyage Autour du Monde,* 1836–9. BMNHN

170 Felipe Guamán Poma de Ayala. Inca girl at work. Drawing, late 16th century

171 Town of Guanuco. *Ibid.*

172 Portrait of Ephraim George Squier. Smithsonian Institution

173 Bridge over the Apurimac River. Engraving from E.G. Squier, *Peru: Incidents of Travel and Exploration in the Land of the Incas,* 1877

174 Hiram Bingham. Machu Picchu's temple of the three windows. Photograph from Bingham, *Report of the Peruvian Expedition,* 1912. BNP

175 The road near Machu Picchu and the Urubamba River. *Ibid.*

176b First site map of Machu Picchu. *Ibid.*

176–7a Typical walls and houses at Machu Picchu. *Ibid.*

177 *Idem*

178 Royal tomb behind the temple of the sun. Photograph

180 Ceramic drum. Musée de l'Homme, Paris

181 Aerial view of the geoglyphs on the plains of Nazca

182 *Idem*

183 Plan and drawings of the Nazca geoglyphs

184 Patrick Mérienne. Map of the Inca empire

Index

Page numbers in italics refer to captions and/or illustrations.

A

Aclla 35, *35, 36–7, 119*
African slaves *104–5*
Agriculture *54*, 59–69, *61, 62, 63*
Ahuasca 35
Alcalde 104
Alguacil 104
Almagro, Diego de 14, 52
Amazon territory 23
Andagoya, Pascual de 14
Andean culture 23, 26; modern 126, 160–2
Andean peoples *14, 15, 54, 61, 106, 107, 126, 127, 168*; beliefs 77; class distinctions 94–7, 104; in colonial times 56–71, *98–9, 100–1, 102–3*; modern 126, 160–2; population 57–8
Andes, *see* Cordilleras
Angelina, Doña 96
Animal husbandry 64, 66, *67*
Animal sacrifice 35, *35, 153*
Antisuyu 23
Apurimac *114*
Archaeological surveys 113–25, 172–83
Argentina 28
Army, Inca 42
Arobe, Don Francisco de *104*
Arriaga, Pablo José de 84
Astronomy 78
Atahualpa, Inca 29, 32, 40, 43–4, 46, *46, 47,* 48–52, *49, 50–1, 92, 93, 131*
Atahualpa, Juan Santos 107
Aucacamyoc 48
Ayllu 67–8
Aymara kingdoms 95

B

Balboa, Vasco Núñez de 13–4

Bingham, Hiram 1–9, 113–6, *114, 115,* 122–5, 174
Bolívar, Simon *108, 109, 110, 111*
Bolivia 65, 70, 97, 107, 110
Bridges 42, *42–3, 173*
Bullfight *104, 105*
Burial, *see* Funerary customs

C

Cacique 67, 79, 94–7, 104, 107
Cajamarca 32, 42, 43–4, 50
Calancha, Father Antonio de *114, 116, 119*
Callao *31*
Canals 61, *68*
Canari *43*
Catari, Tomas 108
Catholicism, *see* Christianity
Caxas 32, 35, 42
Cemeteries, pre-Inca *74, 75*
Chaca suyuyoc 43
Chancay culture *47, 79, 89*
Chan Chan 26
Charles V *28,* 56
Chasqui 32
Chavín culture 26
Chayanta 108
Chicha 46, 64–5, *151*
Chile 23
Chimborazo 19, *90–1*
Chimor 26, 52, 94
Chimú *49*
Chincha 21, 94
Chinchaysuyu 23
Choqqequirau *114, 116*
Christianity 51, 58, 77, *78,* 80–8, *107, 154*; missionaries 48, *72, 73*; native ideas of 73
Chulumani 168
Chuño 62
Cieza de León, Pedro 163
Citua, La, festival 81
Clergy *78; see also* Priests

Coca 61, 62, *62,* 64, *147*
Collasuyu 23
Colombia 16, 110
Colonial administration 55–9, *57,* 95–7, 104–10
Communal lands 64, 110
Concertaje system 110
Conches *66*
Condorcanqui, José Gabriel 107–9
Confession, Inca 88
Confraternities 86
Conquistador 14, 17, 55, *93*
Cordilleras *64–5,* 65
Coricancha temple 52, *82, 83,* 84, 154–7, *155, 157*
Corpus Christi, feast of 80
Corregidor 104
Creoles 110
Cumbi 35, 40
Cuntisuyu 23
Cuzco 22, *23,* 26, 27, 32, 34, *45,* 52, 74, 76, 78, *78–9, 82, 83,* 84, 87

D

Dance of the Lions 90
Dávila, Pedrarias 14
Death cults: native 74, 76–7; Spanish *86, 87*
Death rites, *see* Funerary customs
Drinking vessels 94

E

Ecuador 16, 23, 27, 28, 62, 65
El Dorado 13–21
Encomendero 56–7, 79
Encomienda system 55–7
Engineering, Inca *22, 33,* 61, *68*
Epidemics 158–60
Espiritu Pampa *119*
Ethnic minorities 160–2

F

Feathers *47, 62, 63, 74*
Felipillo 21, 52

Festival of the Dead *86, 87*
Festivals 80–1, *80–1,* 83, *90;* Christian 104–5
Fortresses *22–3, 32–3,* 42, *43*
Four Quarters, Land of the 22–3
Funerary customs and beliefs 50–1, 74–7, *76, 77, 91, 159*; Christian 71, *85*
Funerary doll *88, 89*
Funerary mask *89, 150*

G

Geoglyphs 26, 180–3, *181, 182, 183*
Gold 14, 16, *47, 49, 70,* 116
Guanuco *171*

H

Herbalists and healers 86–7, 88, 90–1
Houses *124*
Huaca 78–84, 91; keepers of 86–8
Huanacauri, Mount 21
Huarachico 21
Huarochiri 107
Huascar, Inca 22, *23,* 29, *29,* 40, 43, 50, 76–7
Huayna Capac, Inca 16–7, 20, 28–9, 52
Huayna Pichu *119,* 122
Human sacrifice 32, 34–5, *45*
Humboldt, Alexander von *90*
Hunting *66, 67*

I

Idolatry, Spanish attitude toward 83–8
Inca civilization: daily life 140–7; European discovery 13–29; idealized depictions *12, 14, 15, 51, 164*; influences on Europe 84

Inca empire 94–5, 108; administration 26–8, 32, 34–5, 43, 67–9; European conquest 31–52, *32–3*, 130–9, *136*, *137*; founding 21–6; history *136*; map *184*
Inca religion 148–57; ceremonies and rites *140*, *149*; eradication of 73–91; myths 62, 64
Incas, Les (Marmontel) *30*, *31*, *37*, *39*
Incas (rulers) 23, *24–5*, 26–7, *26–7*, 44, *45*, 47, 51, 59, *61*, *92*, 93
Incest, royal 47
Indians, *see* Andean peoples
Ines, Doña 96
Ingapirca fortress 43
Inkarri 51
Intihuatana 125, *125*
Inti Rami festival *45*, *153*
Irrigation 61, *68*
Isla del Gallo 17–8

J

Jaguar *89*
James, Saint 81

K

Kero 94
Kinship 69

L

Labor: forced *54*, 56–7, *56–7*, 68, 70–1, 108, *165*, 170–1, *170*; organization of 68–71
Land use 64–9, 94, 110
Law, Inca 34, 38–9
Lima *111*
Llamas 16, 35, *35*, *62*, 64, 66
Llapa, Martín 170–1
Lloque Yupanqui, Inca 25
Lobato de Sosa, Juan 39
Louis XIV *84*
Luque, Hernando de 14

M

Macaws *47*, *62*, *63*

Machu Picchu *112*, *113*, *118–9*, *120–1*, *122–5*, *122–3*, *124*, *174–9*, *174*, *176*, *177*, *178*
Maize 59, 61, *61*, 62, *62*, *63*, *163*
Mamahuaca (goddess) 62
Mama Huaco *26*, *45*, *47*, 62
Manco, Inca 52, 79, 114
Manco Capac *26*, *45*, *47*, *144*
Maps *14*, *15*, *31*, *184*
Marmontel, Jean-François *31*, *37*, *39*
Marriage *47*, 68–9, *68–9*, 85
Maule River 21
Mayra Capac *34*
McNeill, William H. 158–60
Medicine: native 88, 90–1; Spanish 90–1
Mining 70–1, *70*, *71*, 108
Mita 68
Mitimaes 27–8, 65–6
Mochica culture *26*, *27*
Molina, Alonzo de 19, *30*, *31*, 37
Molina, Cristobal de 148–53
Morisco 161
Mulatto 161
Mummies 74, *74*, 76–7
Music 85, *148*

N

Natives, *see* Andean peoples
Nazca culture *26*, *89*
Nazca lines *26*, 180–3, *181*, *182*, *183*
Nobility 94, 97

O

Oca 61
Ollantaytambo 116, *117*
Ondegardo, Polo de 74, 78
Orejóne 20, *21*, *26*
Oroya 43
Otavalo 28
Oxford Analytica 160–2

P

Pacaritambo cave *26*, 62
Pachacuti, Inca 22, *23*

Palca 58
Panama 13–8
Paracas culture *17*, 26, *41*, *74*, *94*
Pasto 21
Peru 23, 65, 97, 107, 110; colonial 55–71, 163, *166*; modern 125–6; pre-Spanish society in 94–5; *see also* Colonial administration
Peru, viceroyalty of 56–8
Philip II 40, *57*
Pisac *60*, *61*, *117*
Pizarro, Francisco 14–8, *18*, *21*, 28–9, 29, 31–2, *33*, 42, 44, 46, 48–52, *52*, 96, *138*; house of *130*
Pizarro, Hernando 44, 48, 50
Pizarro, Pedro 52, 134
Pizarro Yupanqui, Francisco 96
Plants *65*, 66, 91
Polygamy *47*, 69, 85
Poma de Ayala, Felipe Guamán *16*
Potatoes 61–2
Potosí 74, 97, 107
Potosí, Mount 70–1, *71*
Pottery 27
Prescott, William H. 138–9
Priests: Catholic 84–7, *87*; native 86
Priostes 104
Private property 94, *97*, 110
Puberty rites *21*, 85
Pucara 22–3

Q

Quechua language *26*, 69, *69*
Quellca 40
Querna 85
Quinoa 61
Quipu 58–9, *59*, *142*
Quipucamayoc 58, *59*, 67
Quito 20, 28, *39*, 50, 94, 107, *111*

R

Race: mixed *109*, 126, *161*; native 160–2

Regidor 104
Revolts 93, 107–10; modern 126
Roads 32
Rosaspata 116
Ruiz, Bartolomé 16–7
Rumichacas 43

S

Sacsahuaman citadel *22–3*, *32–3*
San Martin, José Francisco de *108*, 110, *110*, *111*
Santo Domingo, Church of *82*, *83*, *157*
Sartigues, Eugène de 116
Schools *97*, *145*
Shawcross, William E. 180–3
Sheep 66
Ships *13*, *16*
Silver *49*, 70, *71*
Smallpox 28, 159
Soldiers: colonial *107*; native *19*; Spanish *18*
Sorcery 86–7, 91
Spain: South American independence from 110
Squier, Ephraim George 172–3, *172*
Stonework *32–3*, 122, *124*
Sucanca 125
Sun cult *12*, 44, *45*, 80, 84
Supay 80
Syncretism 80–1, *83*, 86

T

Taclla 61, *61*
Tahuantinsuyu (Land of the Four Quarters) 22–3
Taqui onqoy 79–80
Tarma 107
Taxes *40*, 68; *see also* Tribute
Temple of the Sun, Cuzco (Coricancha) 52, *82*, *83*, 84, 154–7, *155*, *157*
Temples, Inca *45*
Terraces *60*, 61, *61*
Textiles *17*, 35, 40, *41*, *47*, 68, *74*, *89*, *94*, *128*; workshops for *40*

"Thirteen of the Isla del Gallo" 18–21, *20–1*
Tinta 107
Titicaca, Lake 23, *23*, 26, 62, 64, 94, 95
Titicaca region 26, 62, 64, 94, 95
Titu Cusi, Inca 52, 114
Tiwanaku culture 26
Toledo, Francisco de 58, 69, 107
Topa Amaru, Gabriel 107–9
Topa Amaru, Inca 52, *52, 53*, 107, 114
Topa Yupanqui, Inca *24, 25, 134*

Travel *58*
Trepanation 88–90, *91*
Tribute 32, 67–9, 164–9
Tucumán 28
Tumbes 16, 19, 21, 27, 28, 31

U

Urcu 35
Urubamba Valley *60, 61, 114*, 122, *122, 123, 175*

V

Valverde, Vicente de 48
Vega, Garcilaso de la 28, 140–7

Viceroys *57*
Vicuñas *62*, 64
Vilca 88
Vilcabamba 52, 113, 114, 116, *119*, 122
Vilcañota temple *45*
Villages 57–8, *58*, 104
Viracocha *23*, 83–4
Vitcos 52, 79–80, 113, 114, 116, *116*, *117*

W

Wachtel, Nathan 164–9
War customs, Inca *41*

Waranga 68
Wari culture 26
Weapons: native *19*; Spanish *18*
Weaving 35, 40
Wool *62*
Writing: native 40

X

Xeres, Francisco de 33, 130–3

Y

Yana 94–5, *96*
Yarucpalla, Isabel *39*
Yawar Cocha, Lake 28
Yumbo *101*

Photograph Credits

All rights reserved 16, 17, 35l, 40, 41al, 41bl, 55, 62l, 73, 78, 83a, 85l, 86, 97, 105, 129, 138, 145, 149, 154, 157, 159, 165, 166, 170, 171, 173. Archivo General de Indias, Seville 23, 131, 134, 136, 144. Artephot/Oronoz, Paris 18ar, 18b, 47a, 60, 63, 67, 78–9, 90, 93, 98–9, 100–1, 102–3, 109, 110–1, 132, 148. Artephot/Pestana, Paris 49; Faillet 83b. Arxiu Mas, Barcelona 104–5. Biblioteca del Palacio Real, Madrid 66b. Bibliothèque d'Art et d'Archéologie, Paris 66a. Bibliothèque des Arts Décoratifs, Paris 155. Bibliothèque du Muséum d'Histoire Naturelle, Paris 13, 42–3, 43, 45a, 58a, 58b, 77, 90–1, 94b, 107, 113, 130, 168a, 168b. Bibliothèque Nationale, Paris 28–9, 46, 48, 65, 80–1, 81. Hiram Bingham 114, 117, 122–3, 124l, 124r, 174, 175, 176a, 176b, 177. Bulloz, Paris 61, 64–5, 140, 153. Jean-Loup Charmet, Paris 26–7, 31, 59, 68–9, 108–9. Dagli-Orti, Paris 14, 27, 32–3b, 35r, 44, 47b, 53, 74a, 74b, 74c, 76a, 86–7, 91, 94ar, 95, 96al, 96ar, 96b, 106, 116–7, 118–9, 128, 141, 158, 164, 185. Mary Evans Picture Library 56–7. Explorer/Archives, Paris 57. Explorer/Charmet, Paris 153. Explorer/Desjardins, Paris 21, 79, 88, 89. Explorer/Mary Evans, Paris 110. Explorer/Viard, Paris 112. Fiorepress, Turin 70. Gallimard, Paris 62r, 88–9, 150a, 150b. Giraudon, Paris 15, 19, 70–1, 76–7. Institut des Hautes Etudes d'Amérique Latine, Paris 16–7, 42, 45b. Justin Kerr, New York front cover. Kido 41r, 94al, 142, 180. Loren McIntyre, New York 75, 82, 92. Tony Morrison, Suffolk, England 22–3. Musée de l'Homme, Paris 24–5, 29. Musée du Nouveau Monde, La Rochelle, France 12, 30, 36–7, 38–9, 48–9, 51, 84. Museo de América, Madrid 161l, 161r, 162. Museo San Roque, Buenos Aires 72. Monique Piétri 60, 126. Silvester Rapho, Paris 32–3a, 68, 85; Englebert-BS 126–7; Silvester 127. Roger-Viollet, Paris 20–1, 181, 182, 183. Royal Library, Copenhagen 54. Nick Saunders 123, 125, 178. Smithsonian Institution, National Anthropological Archives, Bureau of American Ethnology Collection 172. Jérôme de Staël, Paris 147

Text Credits

Grateful acknowledgment is made for permission to use material from the following works: William H. McNeill, *Plagues and Peoples,* 1976, reproduced by permission of Penguin Books Ltd, London (pp. 158–60); Nathaniel C. Nash, "Archaeologist Wants to Recover Shrine for Incas," copyright ©1993 by The New York Times Company, reprinted by permission (pp. 154–6); Oxford Analytica, *Latin America in Perspective.* Copyright ©1991 by Houghton Mifflin Company. Used with permission (pp. 160–2); William E. Shawcross, "Mystery on the Desert: The Nazca Lines" (*Sky & Telescope,* September 1984, pp. 168–201). Copyright 1984 Sky Publishing Corp. All rights reserved (pp. 180–3)

Carmen Bernand was born on 19 September 1939, and until the age of
twenty-Wve she lived in Argentina, where she studied anthropology at the
University of Buenos Aires.
Her Wrst Weldwork, conducted in Argentina and Peru, led to her
interest in the Andean peoples. Later settling in Paris, Bernand wrote
a thesis on ethnology under the direction
of Claude Lévi-Strauss, then undertook a study of kinship and depictions of
illness and misfortune in the Ecuadorian Andes, which won her a Doctorat
d'Etat. She currently teaches at the University of Paris X.

Translated from the French by Paul G. Bahn

Project Manager: Sharon AvRutick
Typographic Designer: Elissa Ichiyasu
Editor: Jennifer Stockman
Design Assistant: Miko McGinty
Cover design by Miko McGinty

Library of Congress Catalog Card Number: 93–72812

ISBN 13: 978-0-8109-2894-7

Copyright © 1988 Gallimard

English translation copyright © 1994 Abrams, New York,
and Thames and Hudson Ltd., London

Printed and bound in Italy
10 9 8 7

HNA
harry n. abrams, inc.

a subsidiary of La Martinière Groupe

115 West 18th Street
New York, NY 10011
www.hnabooks.com